EARTH'S AMAZING JOURNEY

T0011170

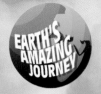

The Amazing Journey from MOSS TO RAIN FORESTS

A Graphic Novel About Earth's Plants

by **Steve Foxe**

illustrated by
Scott Jeralds

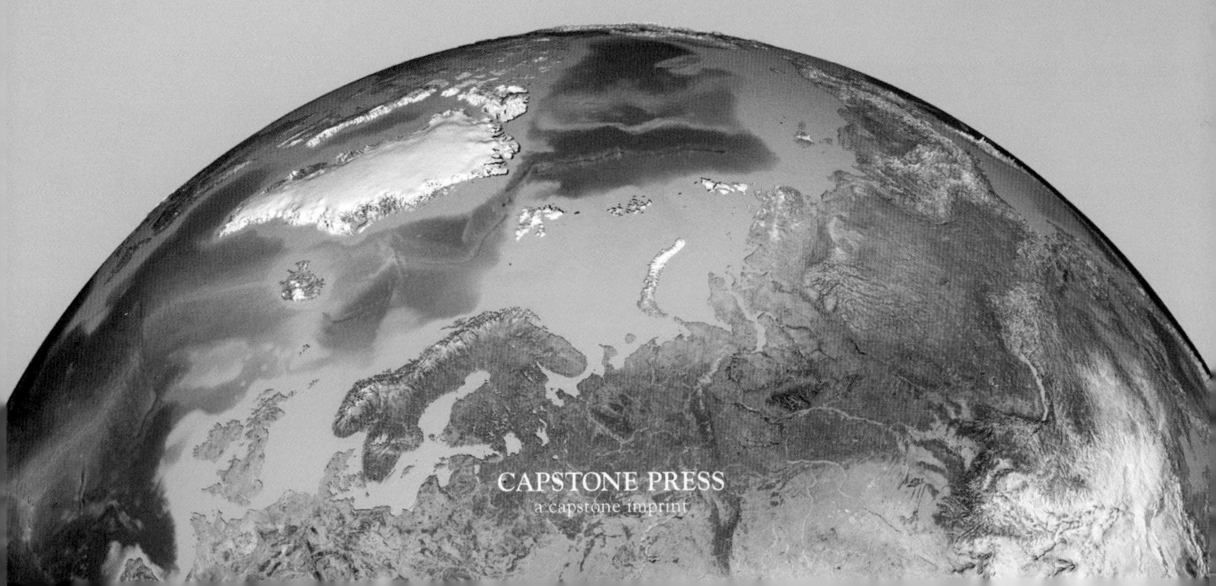

CAPSTONE PRESS
a capstone imprint

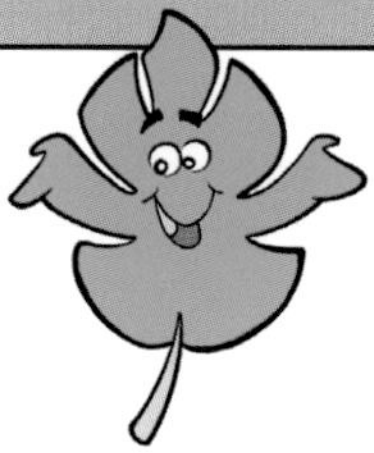

Published by Capstone Press, an imprint of Capstone.
1710 Roe Crest Drive, North Mankato, Minnesota 56003
capstonepub.com

Library of Congress Cataloging-in-Publication Data is available on the Library of Congress website.

ISBN: 9781666393729 (hardcover)
ISBN: 9781666393675 (paperback)
ISBN: 9781666393682 (ebook PDF)

Summary: Explore the origins of Earth's plant life . . . with a talking ficus leaf! In this full-color graphic novel, Leif the leaf takes readers on a magical (and miraculous) journey, revealing how small specks of ancient moss grew into massive rain forests. With laugh-out-loud text and colorful comic book art, this book is sure to sprout any reader's interest in science—and grow their love for planet Earth.

Editorial Credits
Editor: Donald Lemke; Designer: Tracy Davies;
Media Researcher: Svetlana Zhurkin; Production Specialist: Katy LaVigne

Image Credits
Getty Images: Dorling Kindersley, 26 (middle); Shutterstock: Allexxandar, 10 (top), Andrejs Marcenko, 22 (top), anmbph, 16 (top), Artiste2d3d, 13 (middle), Brian A Jackson, 7 (bottom), Catmando, 15 (bottom), Elenamiv, 6, Elliotte Rusty Harold, 21 (bottom), Fotokostic, 27 (top), Harvepino (Earth), cover, back cover, 1, 31, Juan Gaertner, 14, Kichigin, 8, Mauro Rodrigues, 18 (top), noir_illustration (frame around Graphic Novel), cover, 1, P Kyriakos, 16 (bottom left), Robi_Create (logo background), cover, back cover, 1, Ryoko Fujiwara, 10 (bottom right), Shawn Hempel, 9 (top right), Uwe Bergwitz, 24–25 (back), Vitalii_Mamchuk, 18 (bottom), Yeinism, 27 (bottom)

All internet sites appearing in back matter were available and accurate when this book was sent to press.

Printed and bound in the USA. 5195

Table of Contents

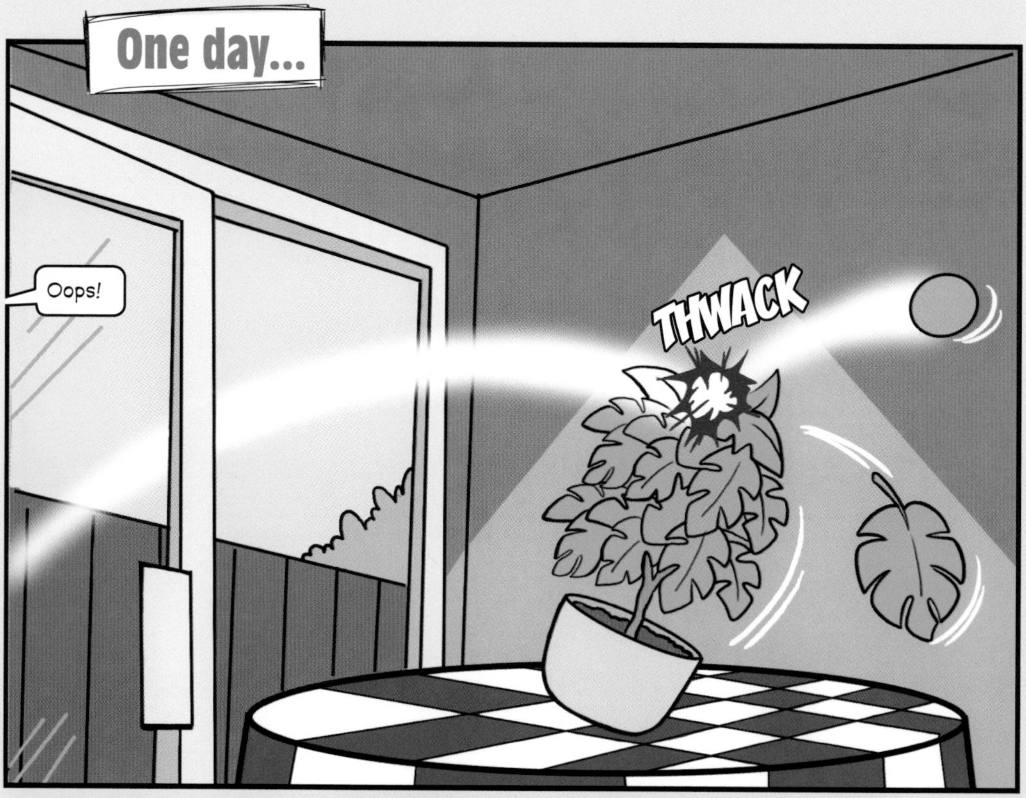
One day...
Oops!
THWACK

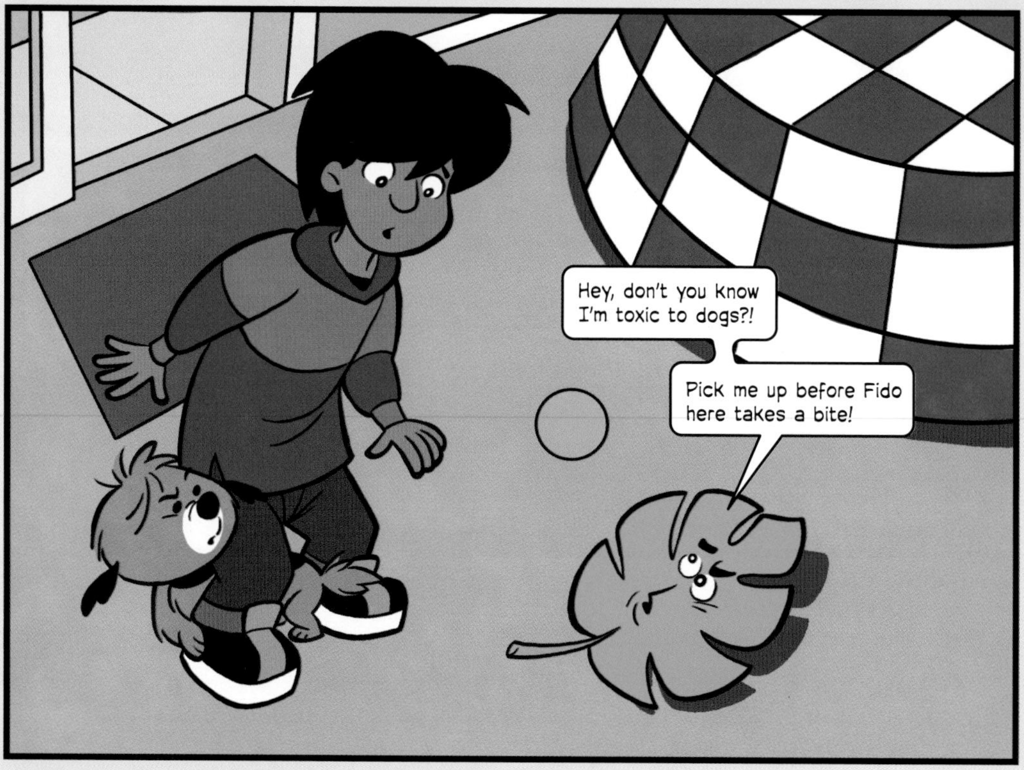
Hey, don't you know I'm toxic to dogs?!
Pick me up before Fido here takes a bite!

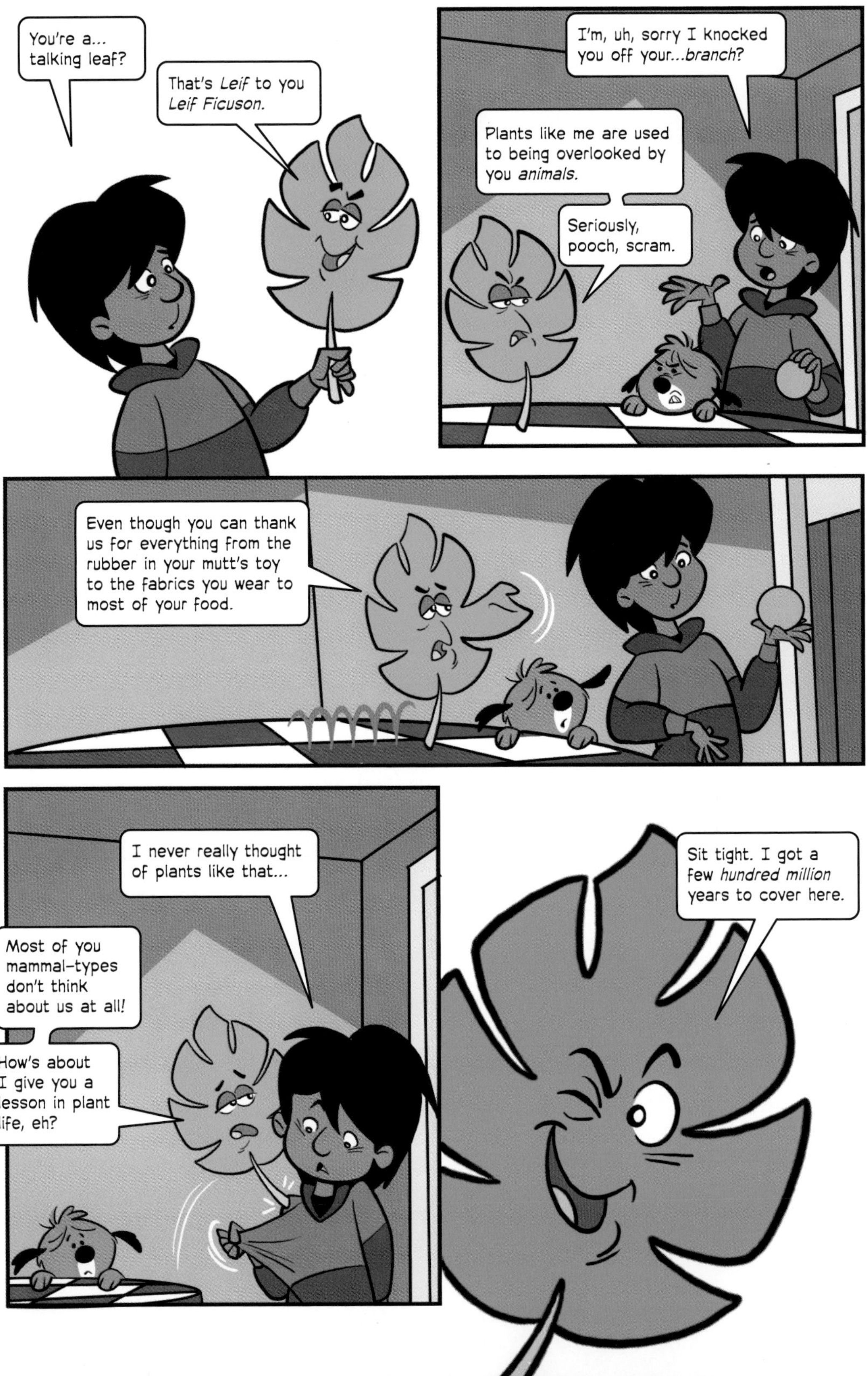
You're a... talking leaf?
That's *Leif* to you *Leif Ficuson.*
I'm, uh, sorry I knocked you off your...*branch*?
Plants like me are used to being overlooked by you *animals.*
Seriously, pooch, scram.
Even though you can thank us for everything from the rubber in your mutt's toy to the fabrics you wear to most of your food.
I never really thought of plants like that...
Most of you mammal-types don't think about us at all!
How's about I give you a lesson in plant life, eh?
Sit tight. I got a few *hundred million* years to cover here.

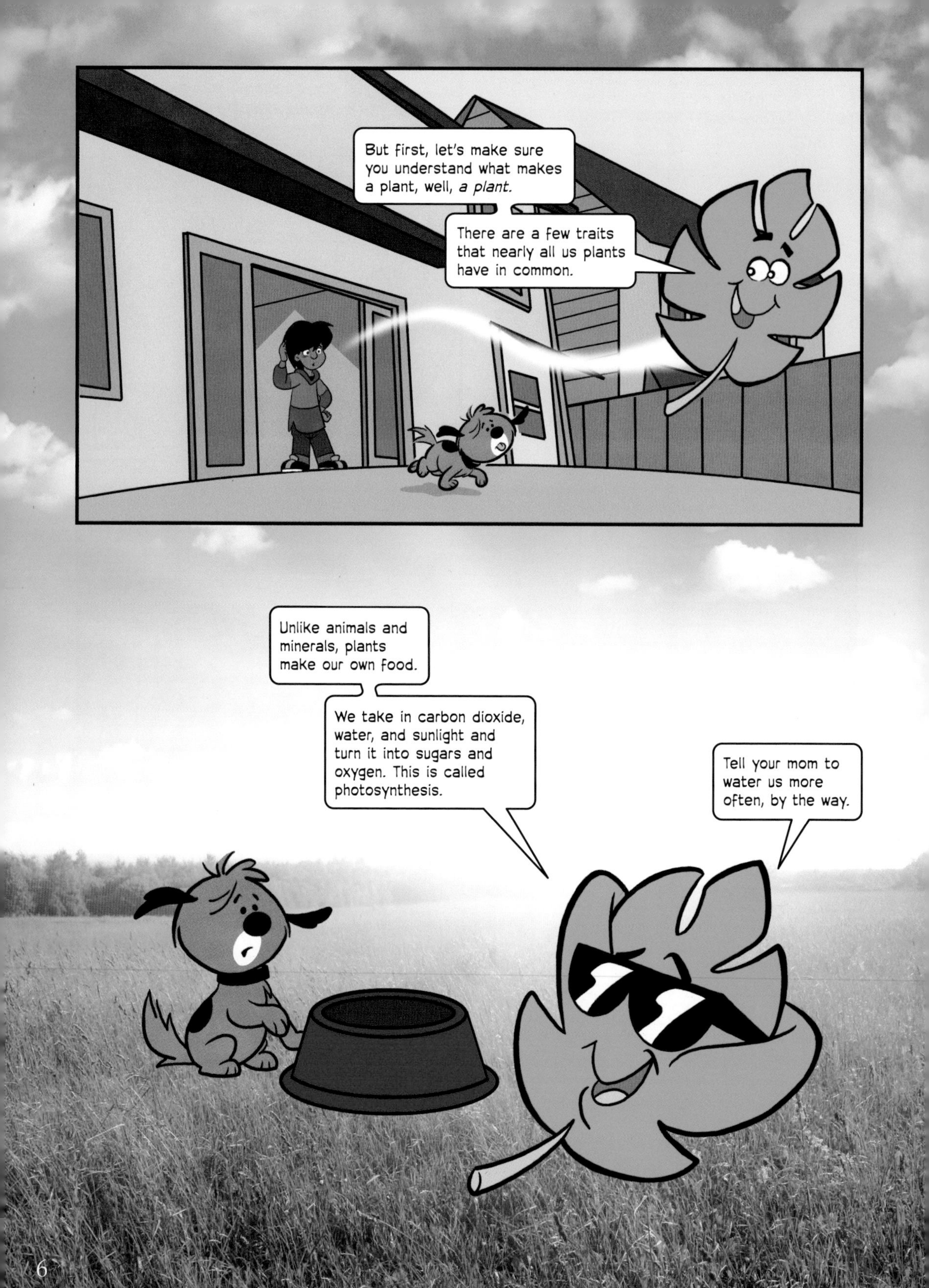

But first, let's make sure you understand what makes a plant, well, *a plant.*
There are a few traits that nearly all us plants have in common.
Unlike animals and minerals, plants make our own food.
We take in carbon dioxide, water, and sunlight and turn it into sugars and oxygen. This is called photosynthesis.
Tell your mom to water us more often, by the way.

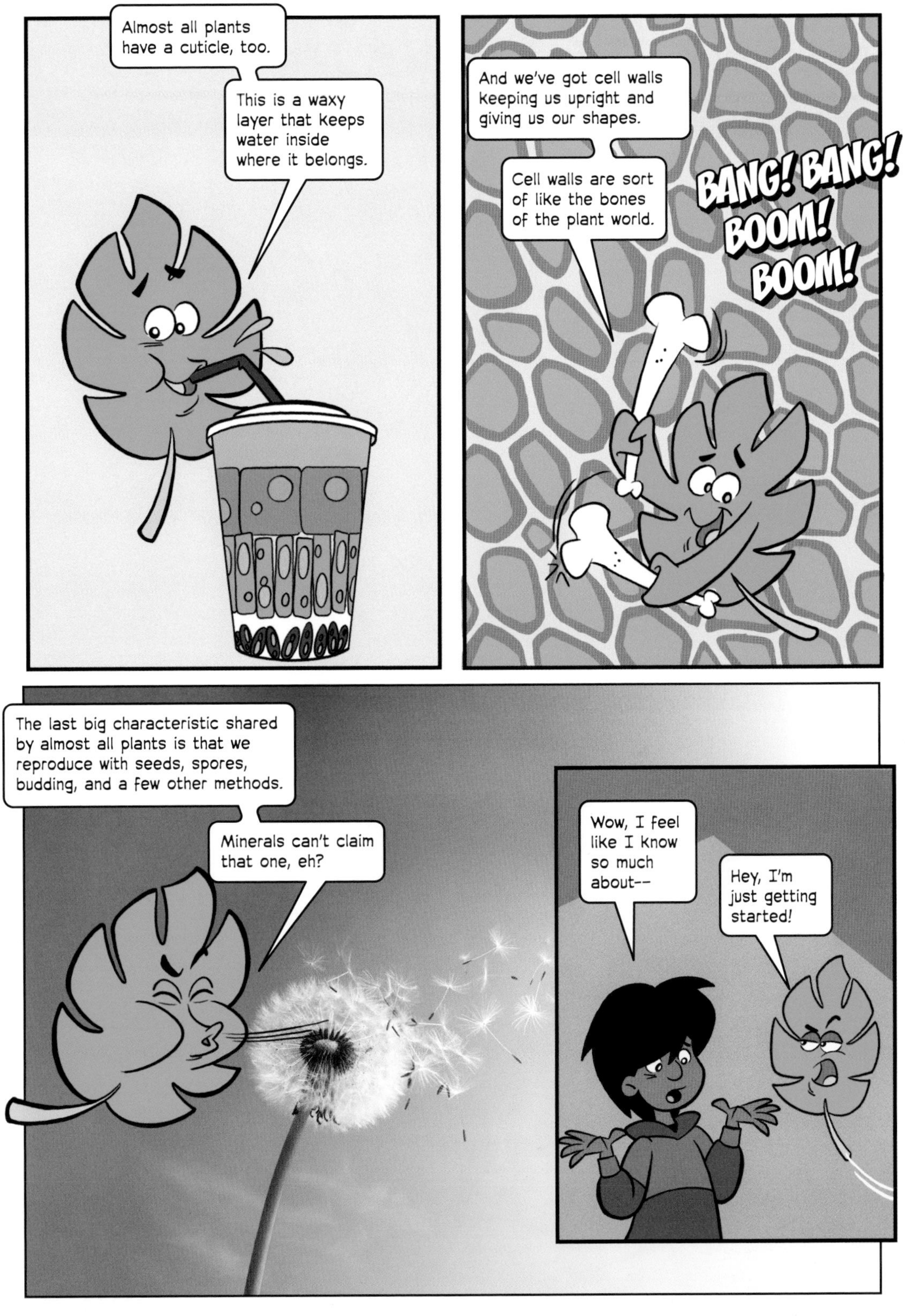
Almost all plants have a cuticle, too.
This is a waxy layer that keeps water inside where it belongs.
And we've got cell walls keeping us upright and giving us our shapes.
Cell walls are sort of like the bones of the plant world.
BANG! BANG! BOOM! BOOM!
The last big characteristic shared by almost all plants is that we reproduce with seeds, spores, budding, and a few other methods.
Minerals can't claim that one, eh?
Wow, I feel like I know so much about--
Hey, I'm just getting started!

Chapter 1: THE EARLIEST PLANTS

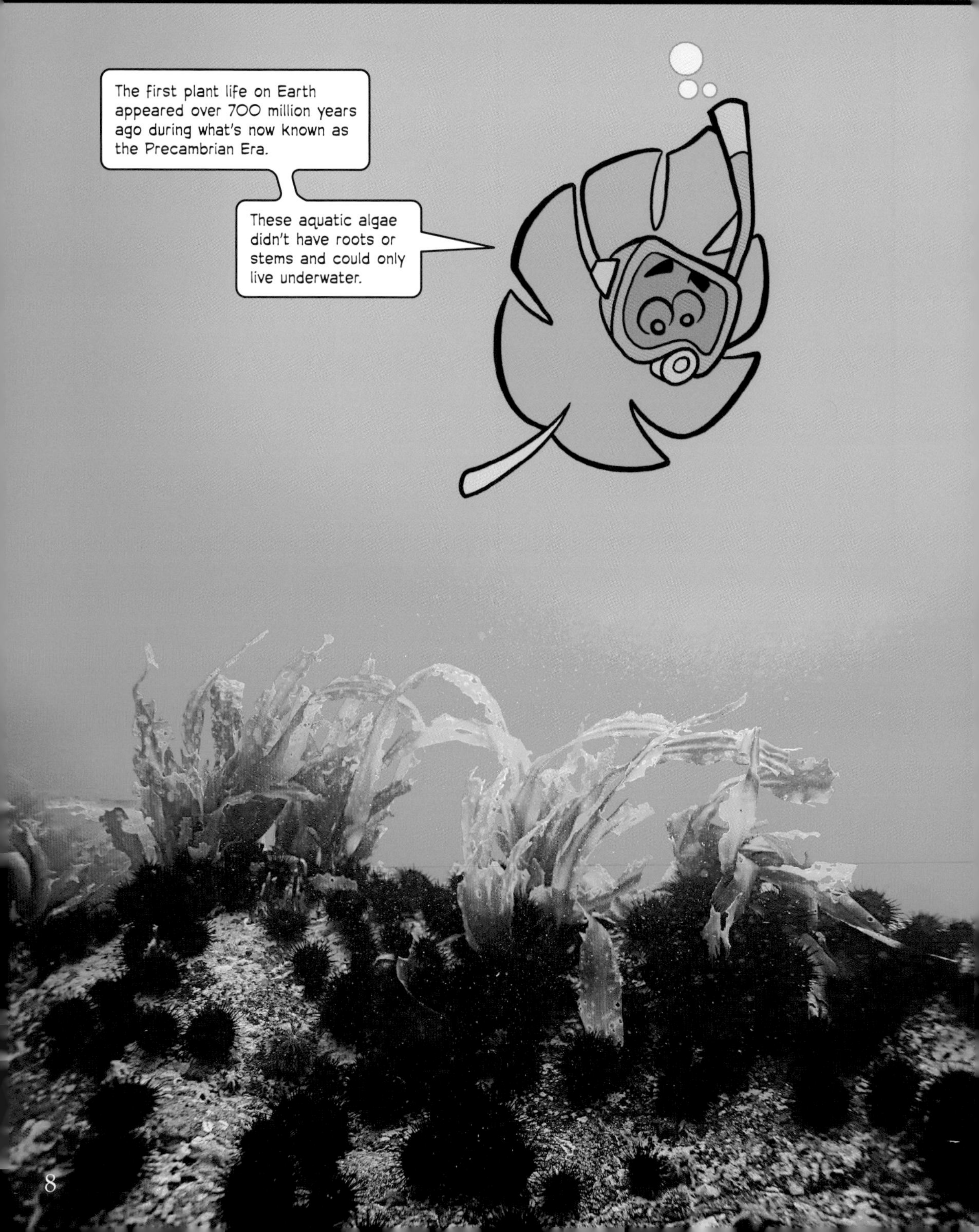

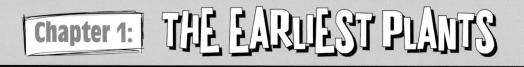

The first plant life on Earth appeared over 700 million years ago during what's now known as the Precambrian Era.
These aquatic algae didn't have roots or stems and could only live underwater.

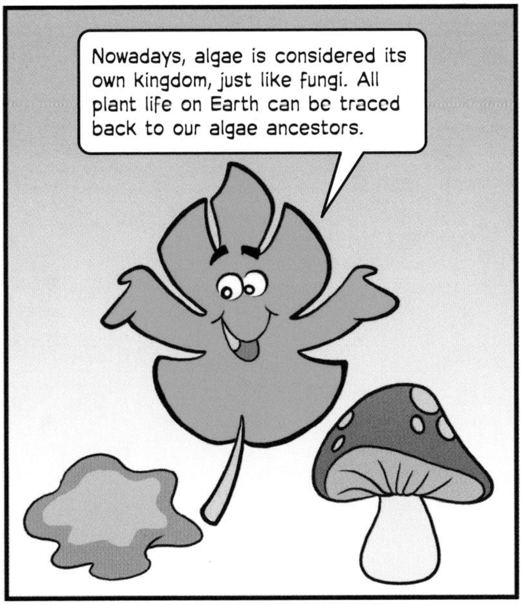
Nowadays, algae is considered its own kingdom, just like fungi. All plant life on Earth can be traced back to our algae ancestors.

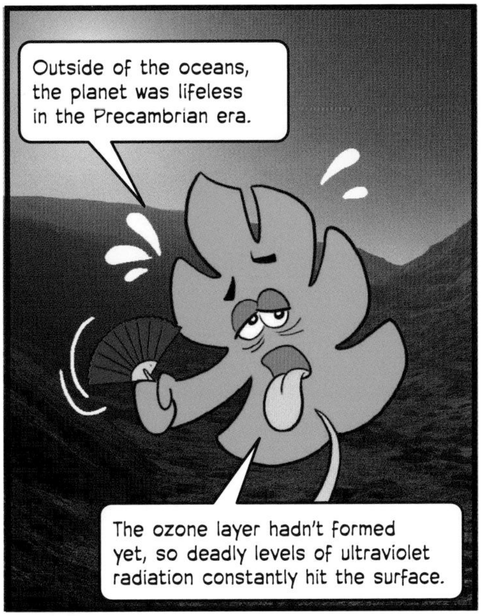
Outside of the oceans, the planet was lifeless in the Precambrian era.
The ozone layer hadn't formed yet, so deadly levels of ultraviolet radiation constantly hit the surface.

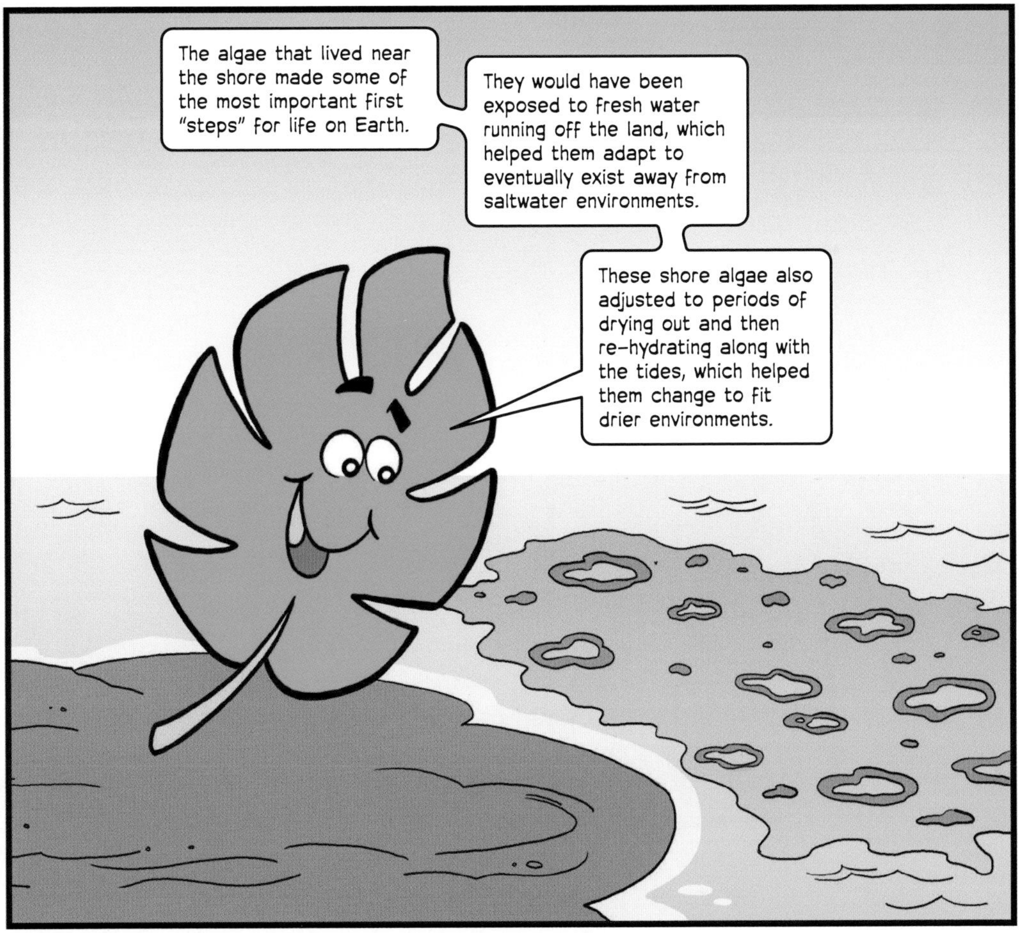
The algae that lived near the shore made some of the most important first "steps" for life on Earth.
They would have been exposed to fresh water running off the land, which helped them adapt to eventually exist away from saltwater environments.
These shore algae also adjusted to periods of drying out and then re-hydrating along with the tides, which helped them change to fit drier environments.

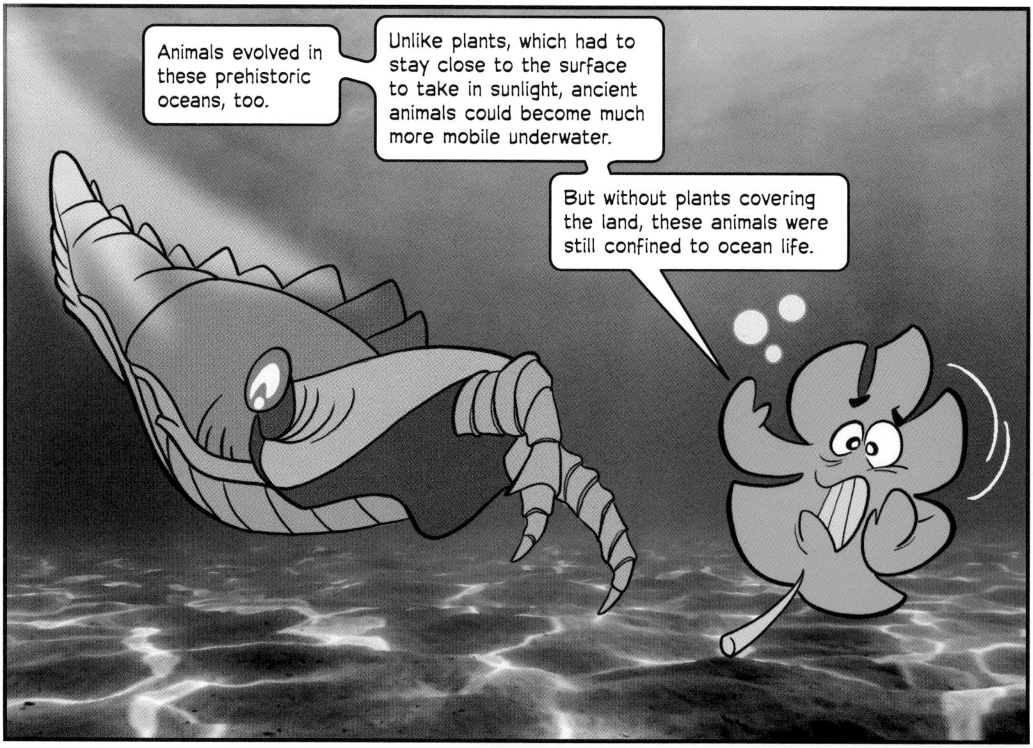
Animals evolved in these prehistoric oceans, too.
Unlike plants, which had to stay close to the surface to take in sunlight, ancient animals could become much more mobile underwater.
But without plants covering the land, these animals were still confined to ocean life.

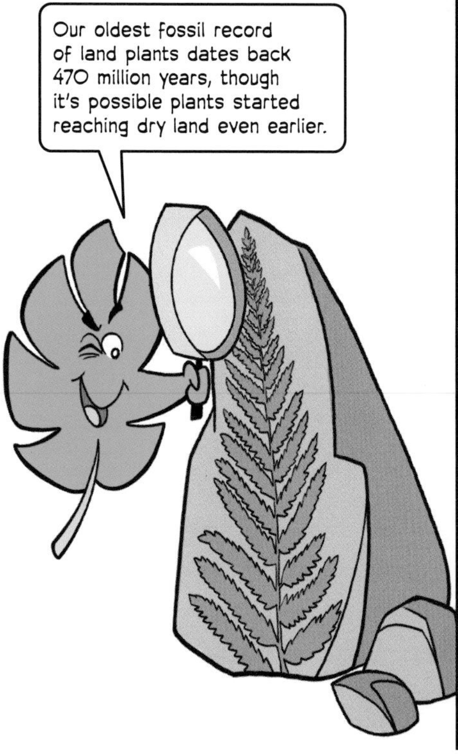
Our oldest fossil record of land plants dates back 470 million years, though it's possible plants started reaching dry land even earlier.

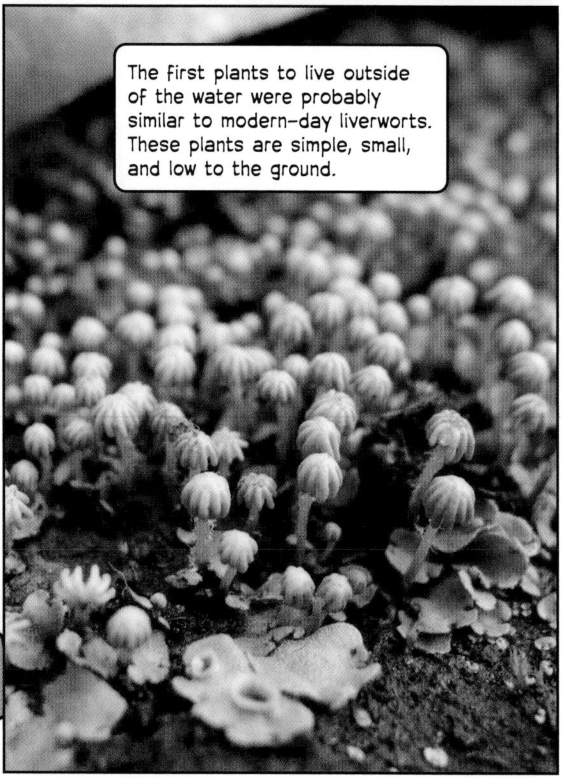
The first plants to live outside of the water were probably similar to modern-day liverworts. These plants are simple, small, and low to the ground.

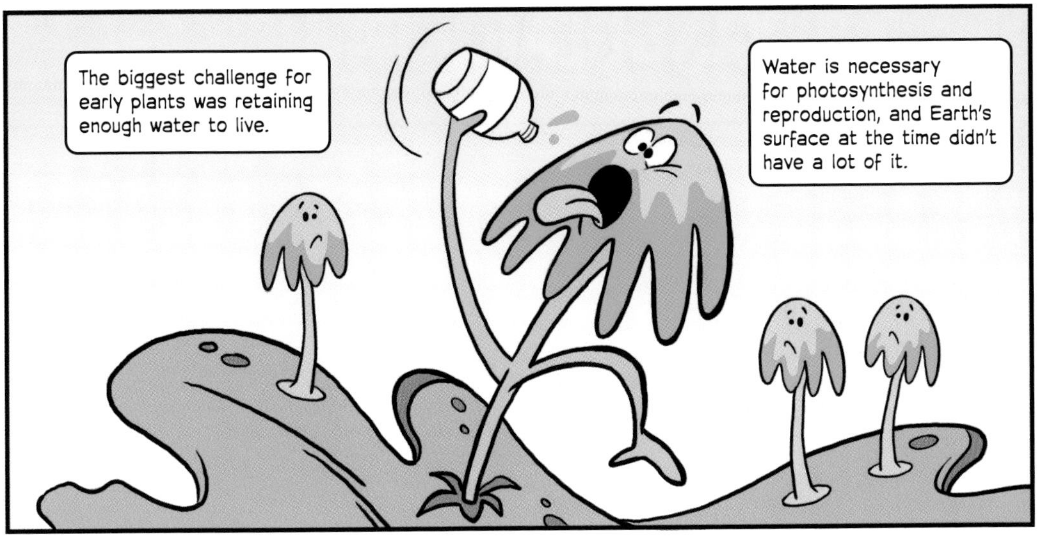
The biggest challenge for early plants was retaining enough water to live.
Water is necessary for photosynthesis and reproduction, and Earth's surface at the time didn't have a lot of it.

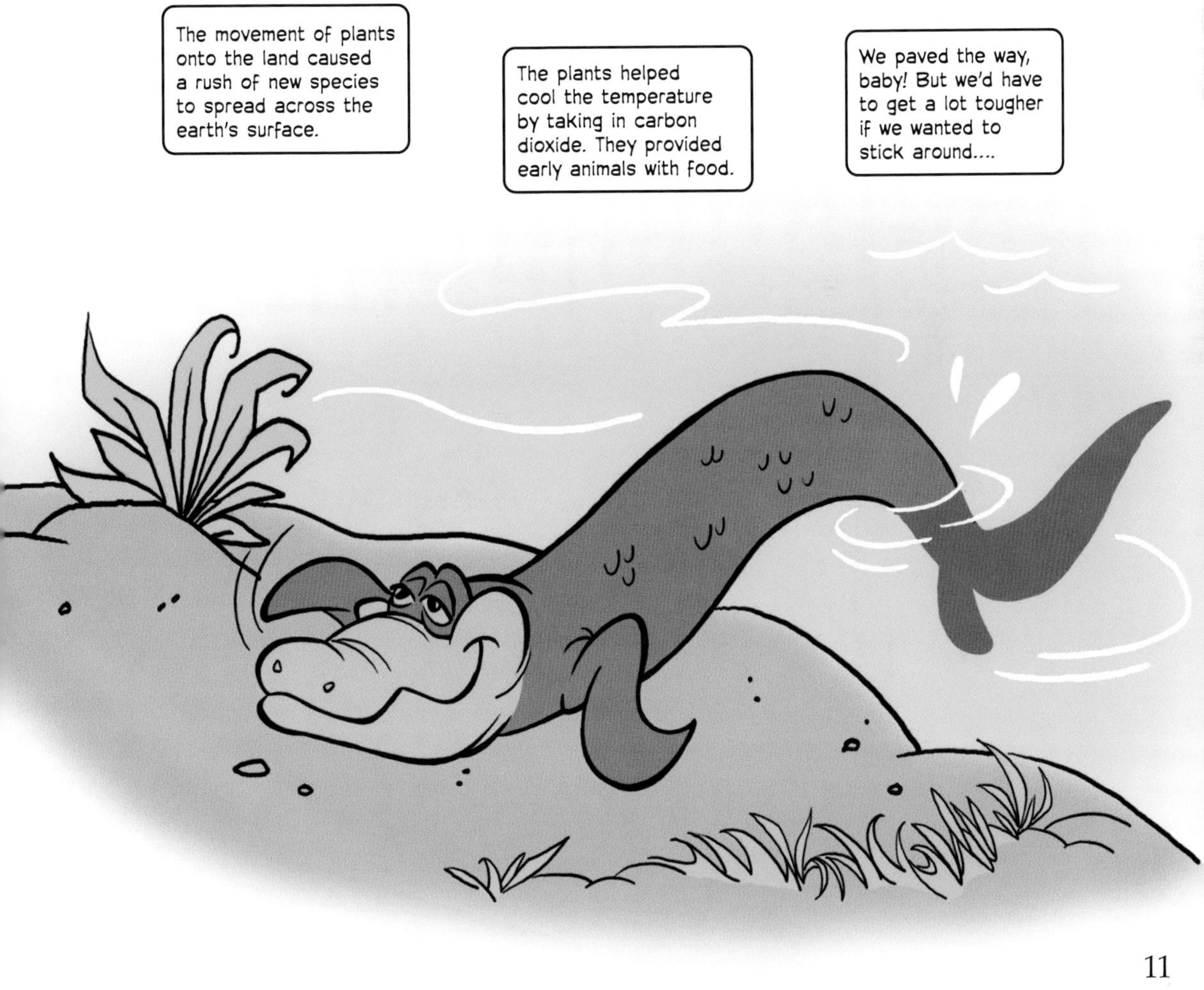
The movement of plants onto the land caused a rush of new species to spread across the earth's surface.
The plants helped cool the temperature by taking in carbon dioxide. They provided early animals with food.
We paved the way, baby! But we'd have to get a lot tougher if we wanted to stick around....

Chapter 2: VASCULAR PLANTS

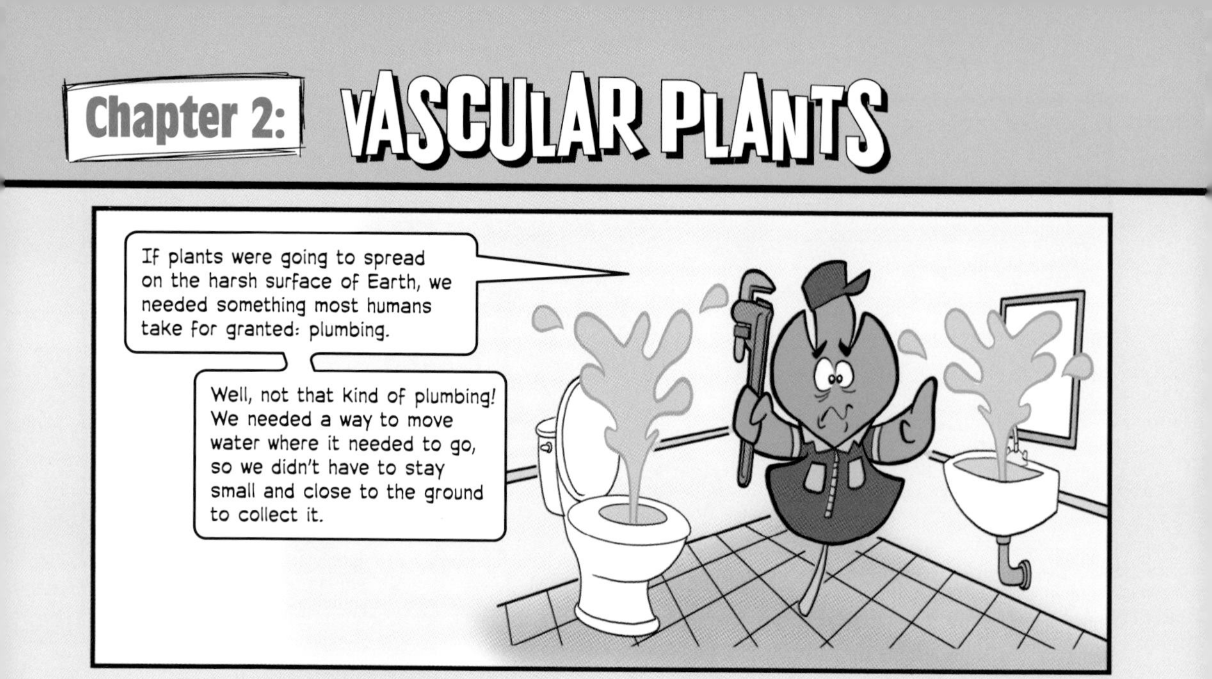

If plants were going to spread on the harsh surface of Earth, we needed something most humans take for granted: plumbing.
Well, not that kind of plumbing! We needed a way to move water where it needed to go, so we didn't have to stay small and close to the ground to collect it.

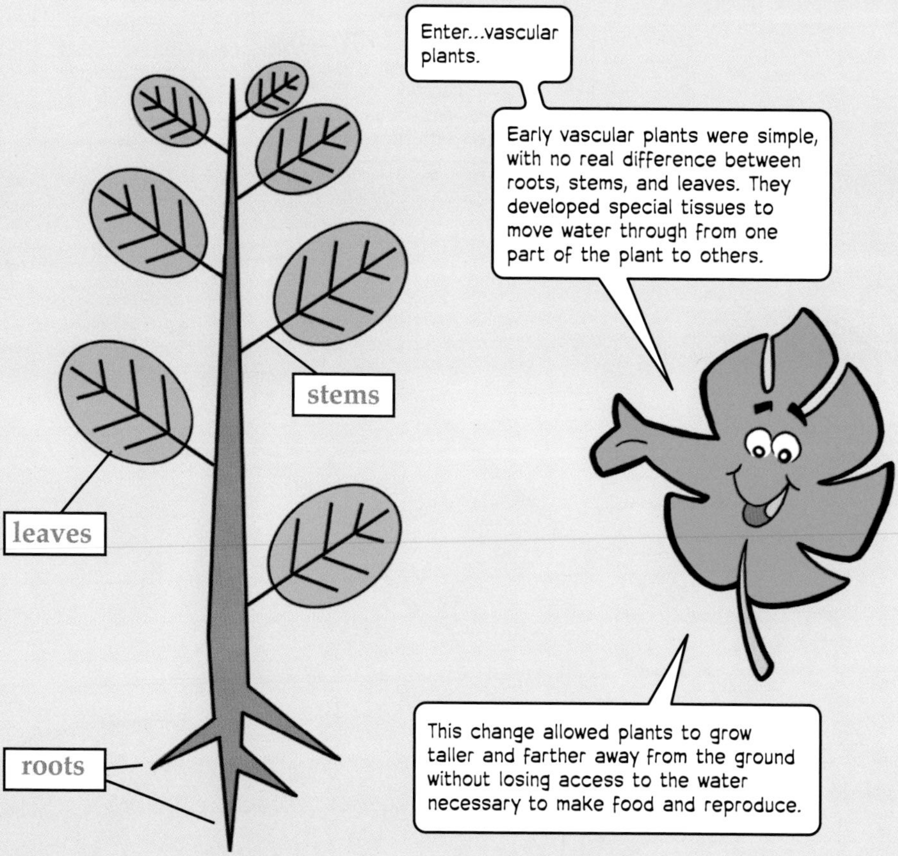

Enter...vascular plants.
Early vascular plants were simple, with no real difference between roots, stems, and leaves. They developed special tissues to move water through from one part of the plant to others.
stems
leaves
roots
This change allowed plants to grow taller and farther away from the ground without losing access to the water necessary to make food and reproduce.

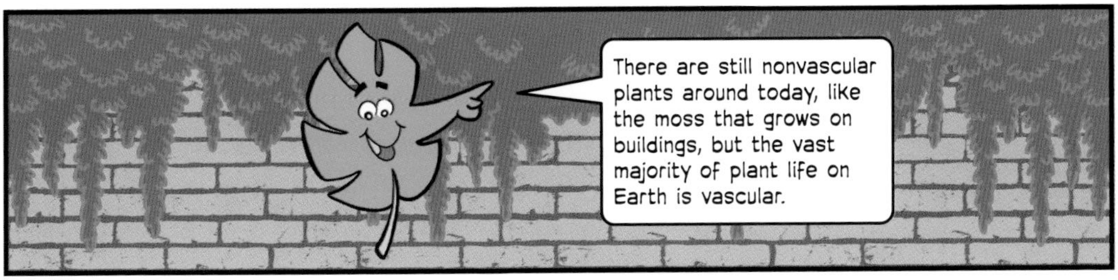
There are still nonvascular plants around today, like the moss that grows on buildings, but the vast majority of plant life on Earth is vascular.

Some of the earliest vascular plants were ferns, which still exist.

Vascular plants like these ferns collect water from the roots under the soil. They move it through the stem and into the leaves, which help take in sunlight for photosynthesis.

The same vascular system also distributes sugars--the result of photosynthesis--through the plant, keeping the cycle going.

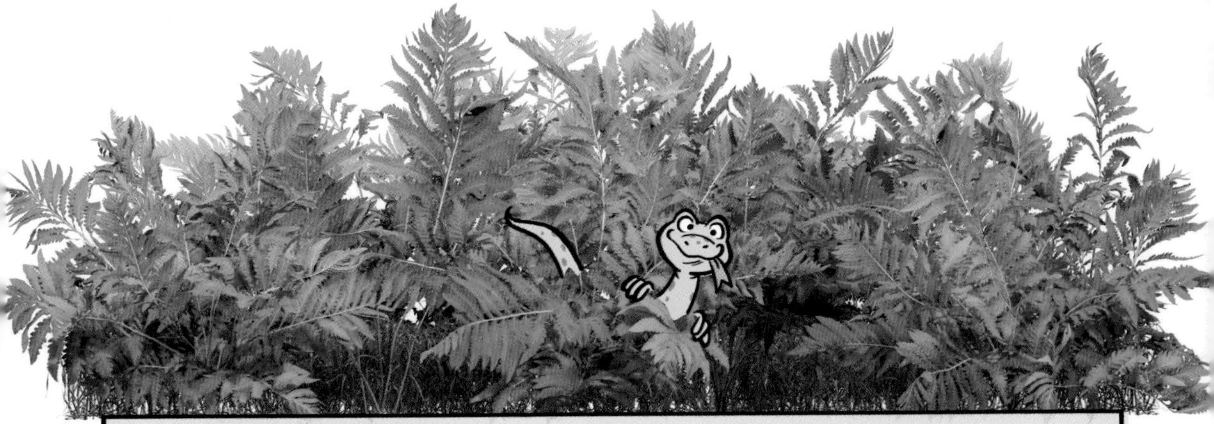

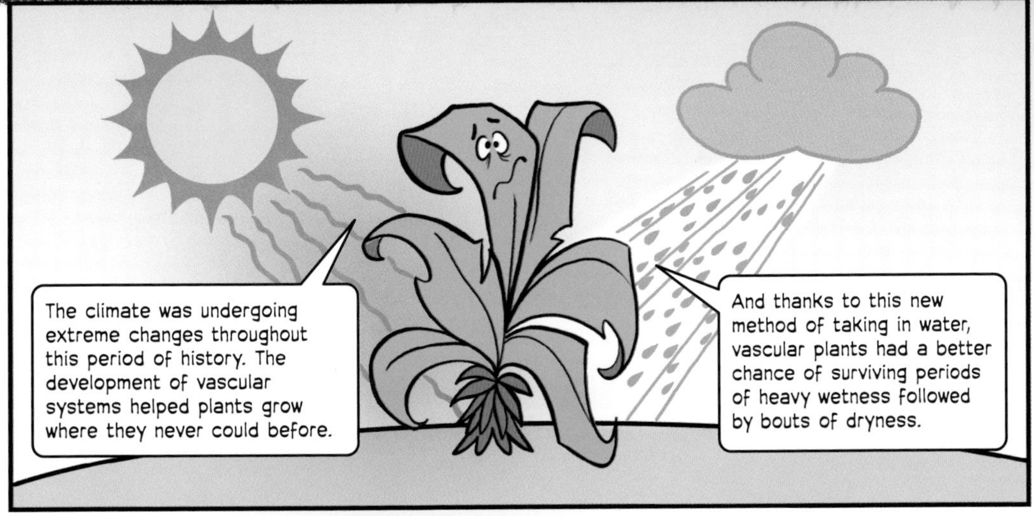
The climate was undergoing extreme changes throughout this period of history. The development of vascular systems helped plants grow where they never could before.
And thanks to this new method of taking in water, vascular plants had a better chance of surviving periods of heavy wetness followed by bouts of dryness.

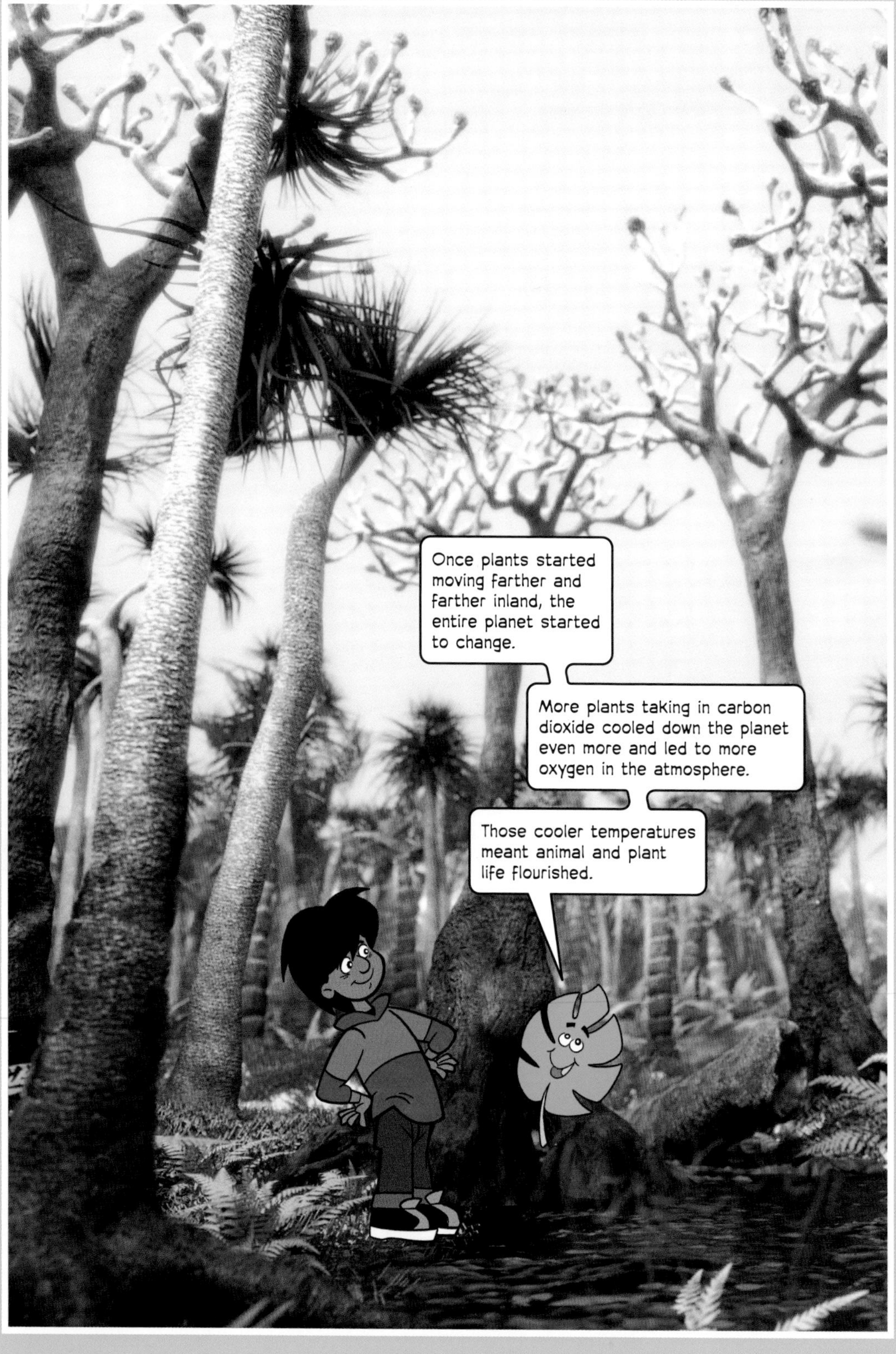
Once plants started moving farther and farther inland, the entire planet started to change.
More plants taking in carbon dioxide cooled down the planet even more and led to more oxygen in the atmosphere.
Those cooler temperatures meant animal and plant life flourished.

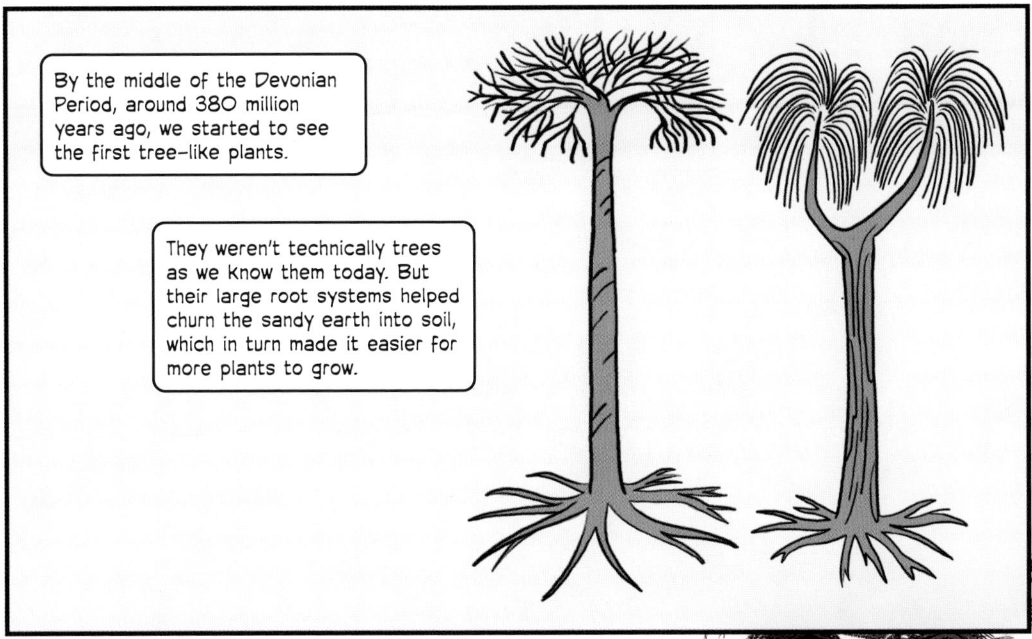
By the middle of the Devonian Period, around 380 million years ago, we started to see the first tree-like plants.
They weren't technically trees as we know them today. But their large root systems helped churn the sandy earth into soil, which in turn made it easier for more plants to grow.

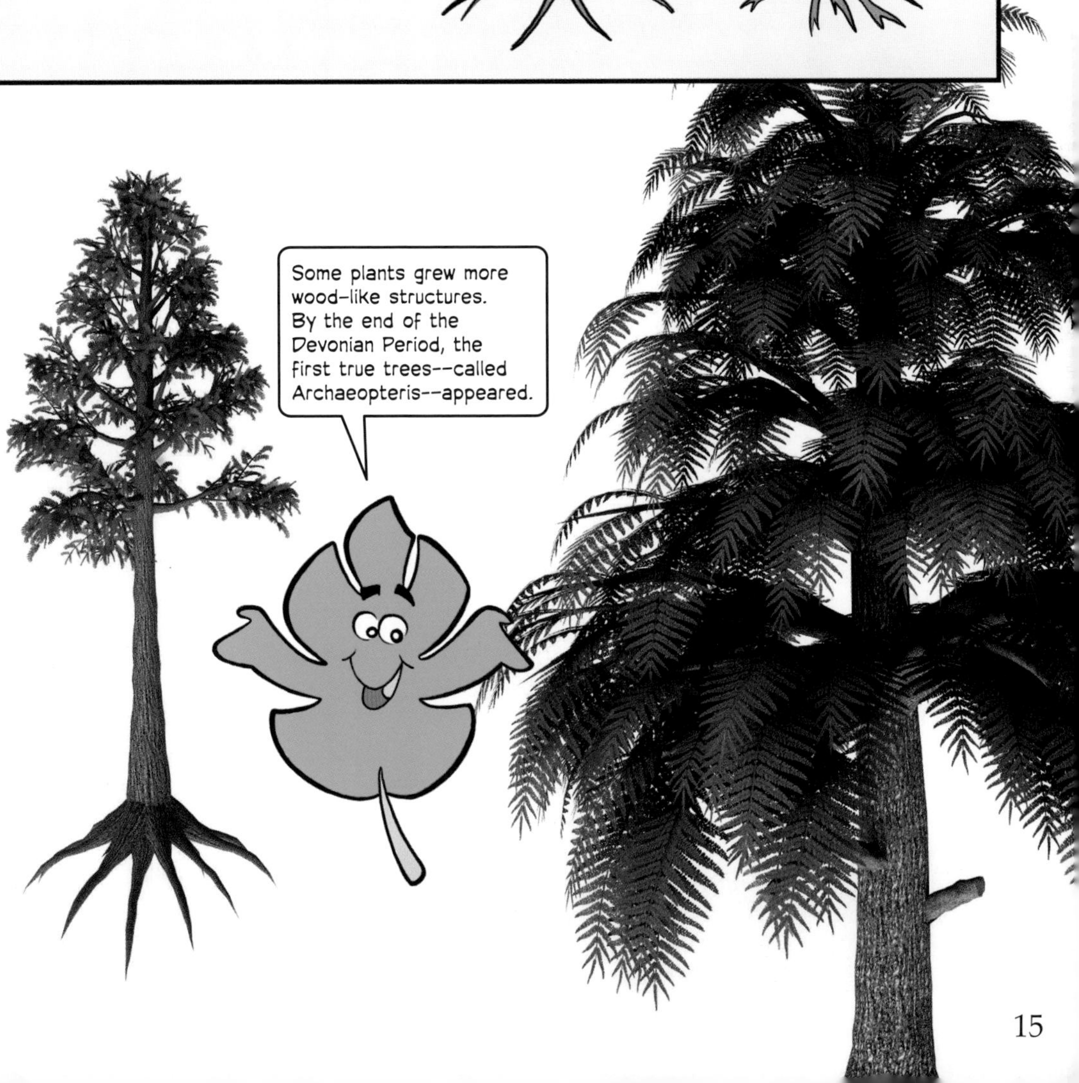
Some plants grew more wood-like structures. By the end of the Devonian Period, the first true trees--called Archaeopteris--appeared.

Chapter 3: SEEDS

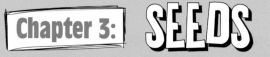

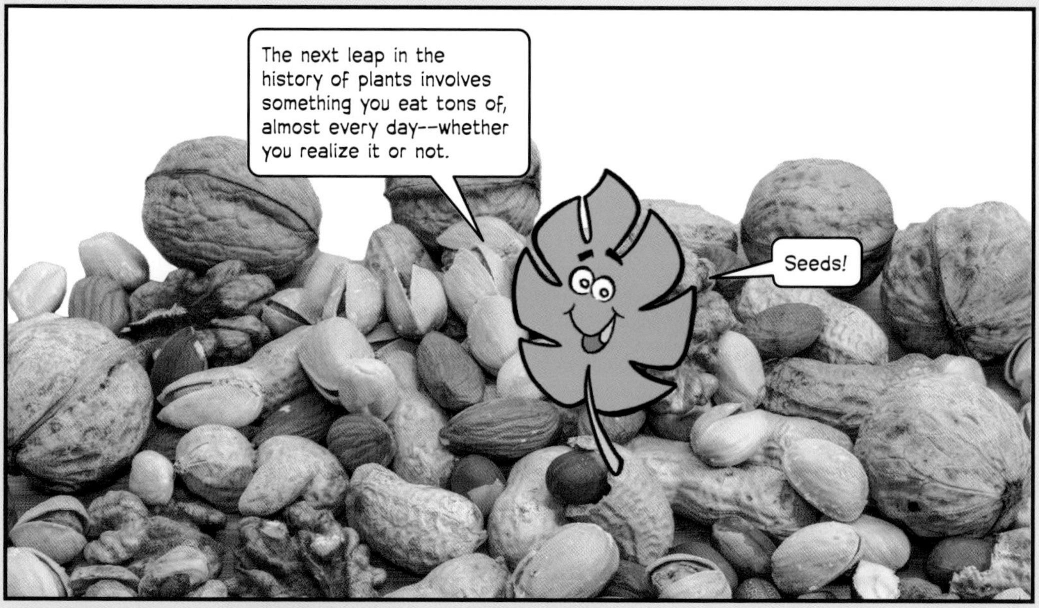
The next leap in the history of plants involves something you eat tons of, almost every day--whether you realize it or not.
Seeds!

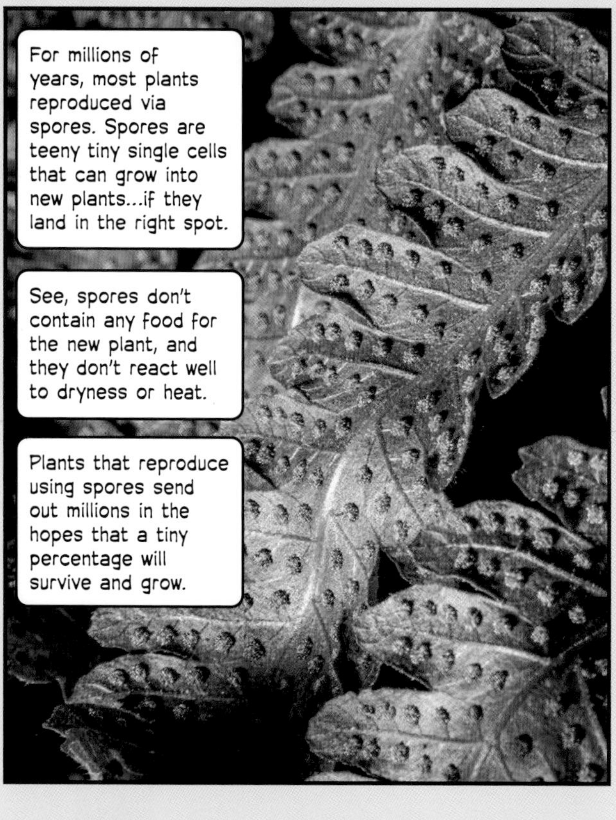
For millions of years, most plants reproduced via spores. Spores are teeny tiny single cells that can grow into new plants...if they land in the right spot.
See, spores don't contain any food for the new plant, and they don't react well to dryness or heat.
Plants that reproduce using spores send out millions in the hopes that a tiny percentage will survive and grow.

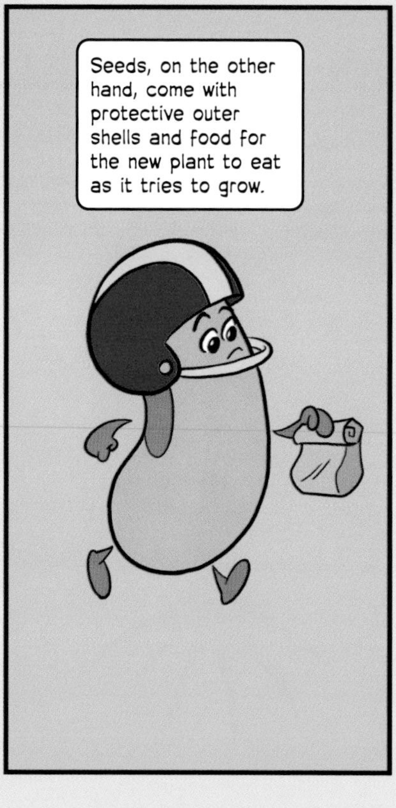
Seeds, on the other hand, come with protective outer shells and food for the new plant to eat as it tries to grow.

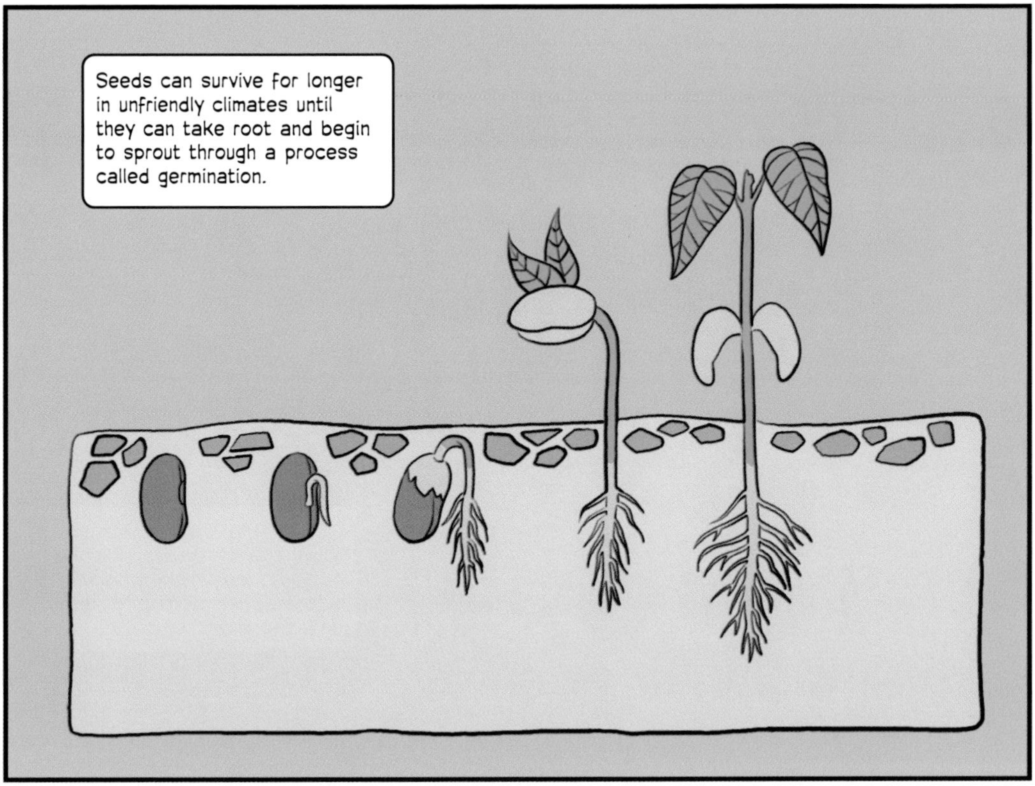
Seeds can survive for longer in unfriendly climates until they can take root and begin to sprout through a process called germination.

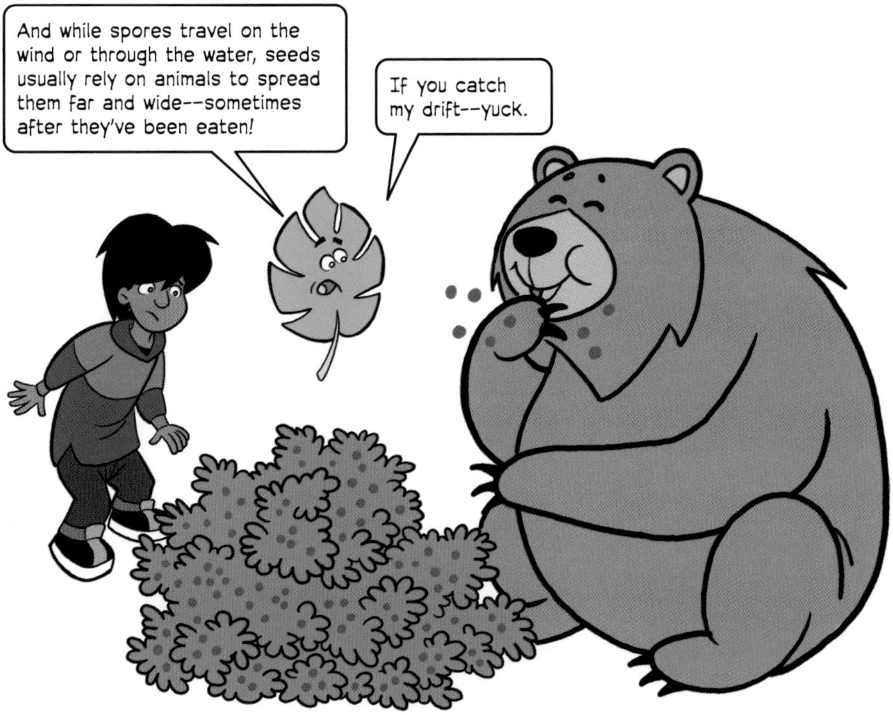
And while spores travel on the wind or through the water, seeds usually rely on animals to spread them far and wide--sometimes after they've been eaten!
If you catch my drift--yuck.

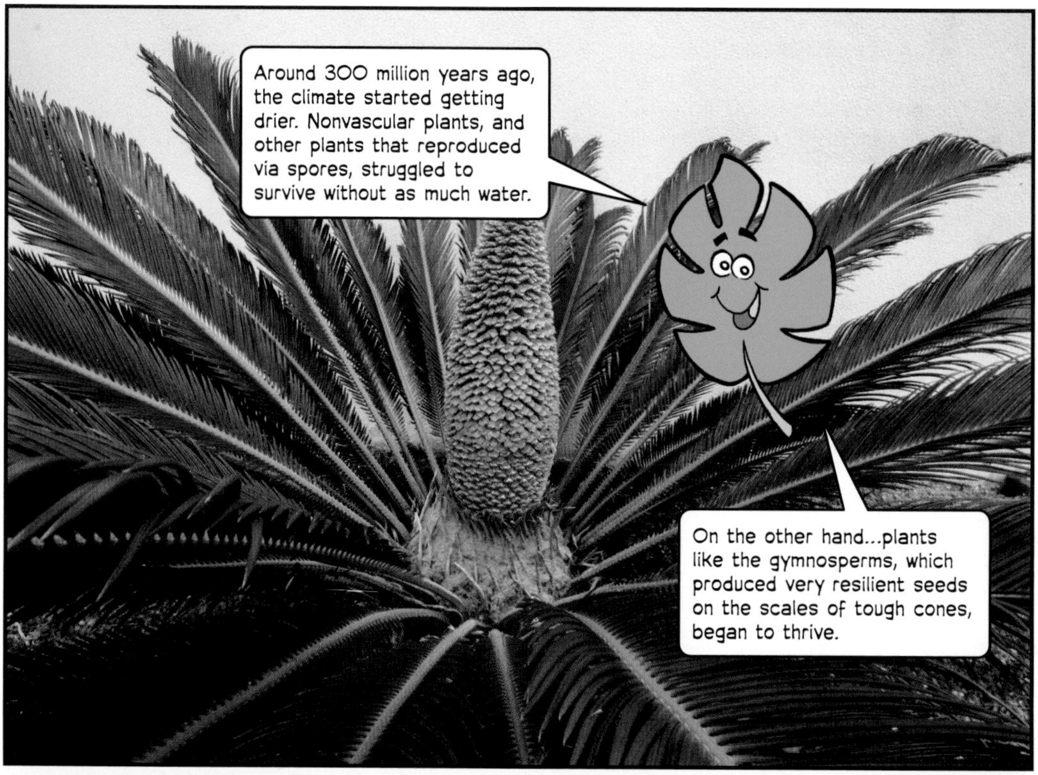
Around 300 million years ago, the climate started getting drier. Nonvascular plants, and other plants that reproduced via spores, struggled to survive without as much water.
On the other hand...plants like the gymnosperms, which produced very resilient seeds on the scales of tough cones, began to thrive.

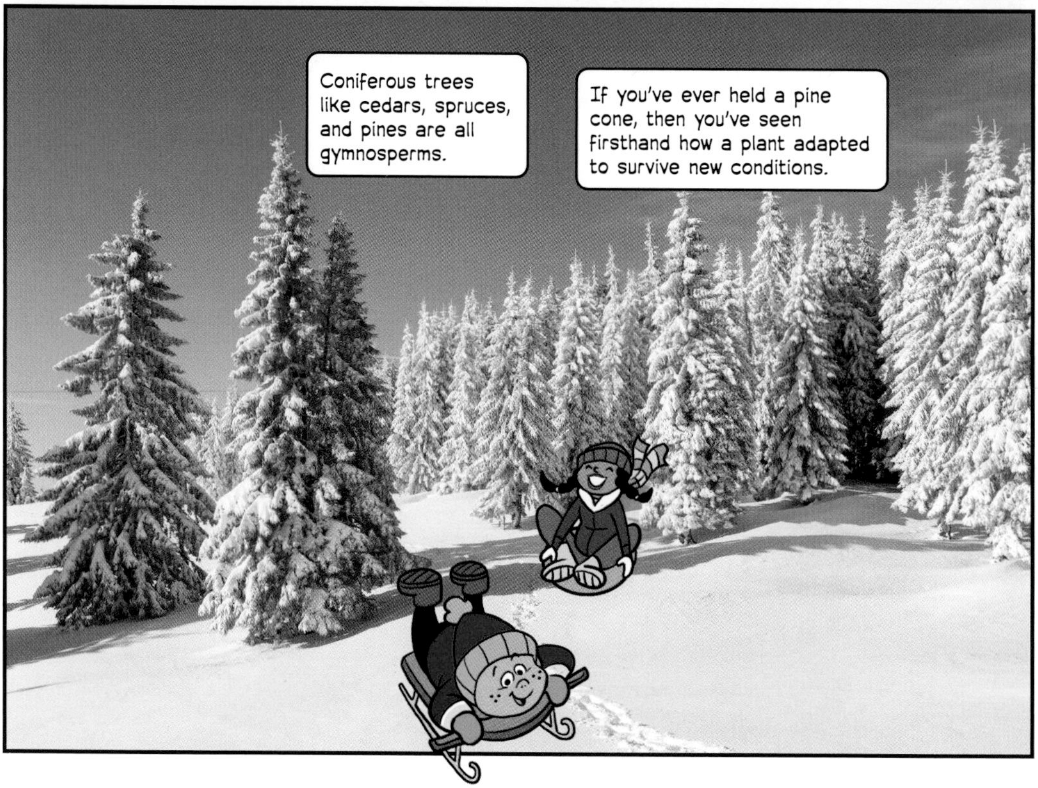
Coniferous trees like cedars, spruces, and pines are all gymnosperms.
If you've ever held a pine cone, then you've seen firsthand how a plant adapted to survive new conditions.

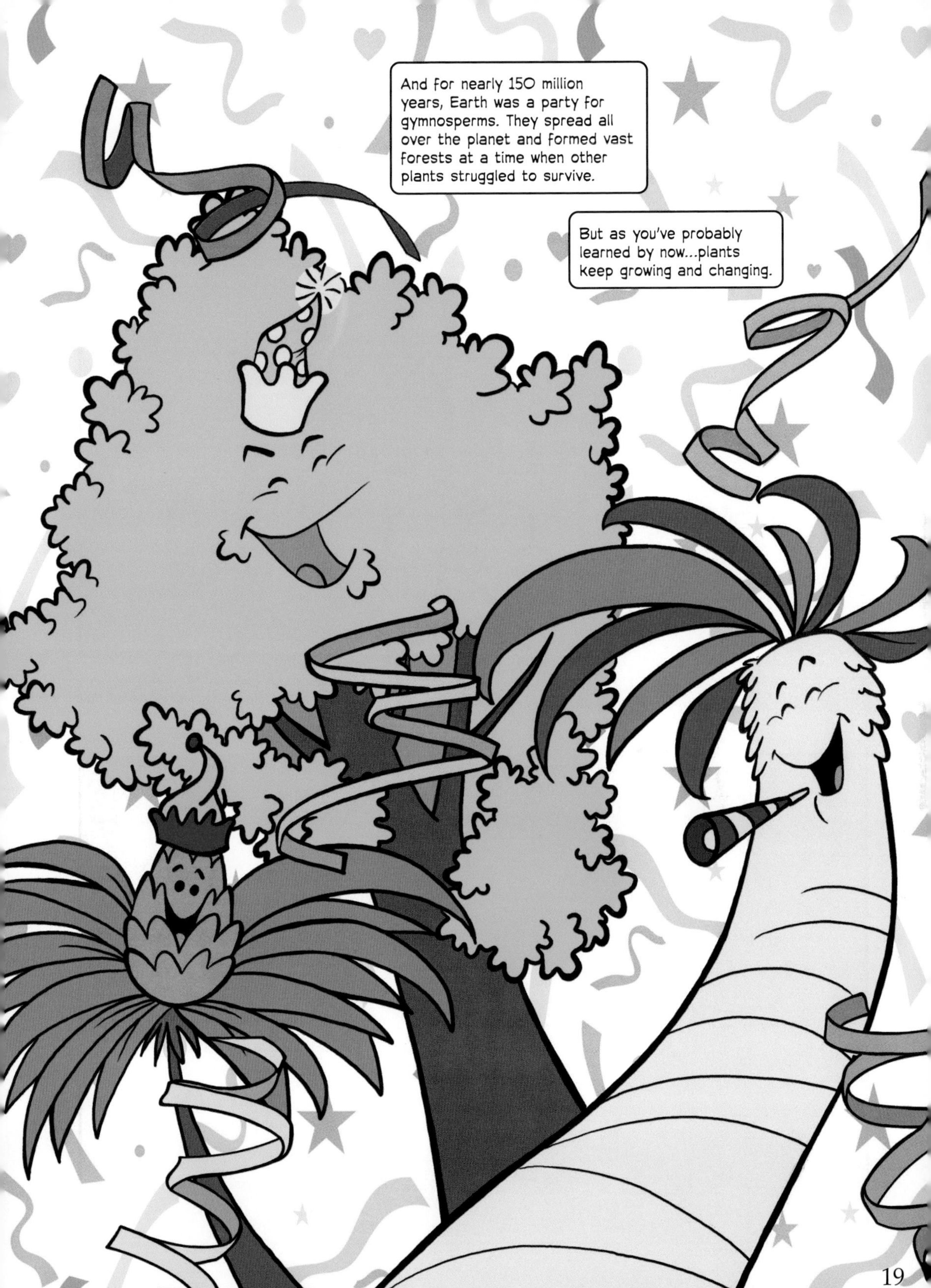
And for nearly 150 million years, Earth was a party for gymnosperms. They spread all over the planet and formed vast forests at a time when other plants struggled to survive.
But as you've probably learned by now...plants keep growing and changing.

Chapter 4: FLOWERS BLOOM

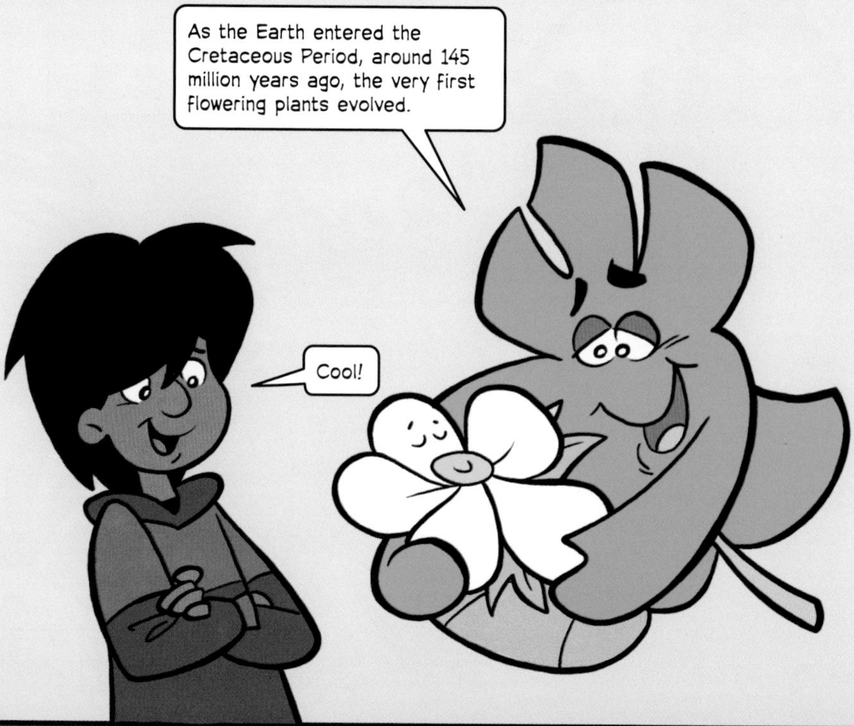
As the Earth entered the Cretaceous Period, around 145 million years ago, the very first flowering plants evolved.
Cool!

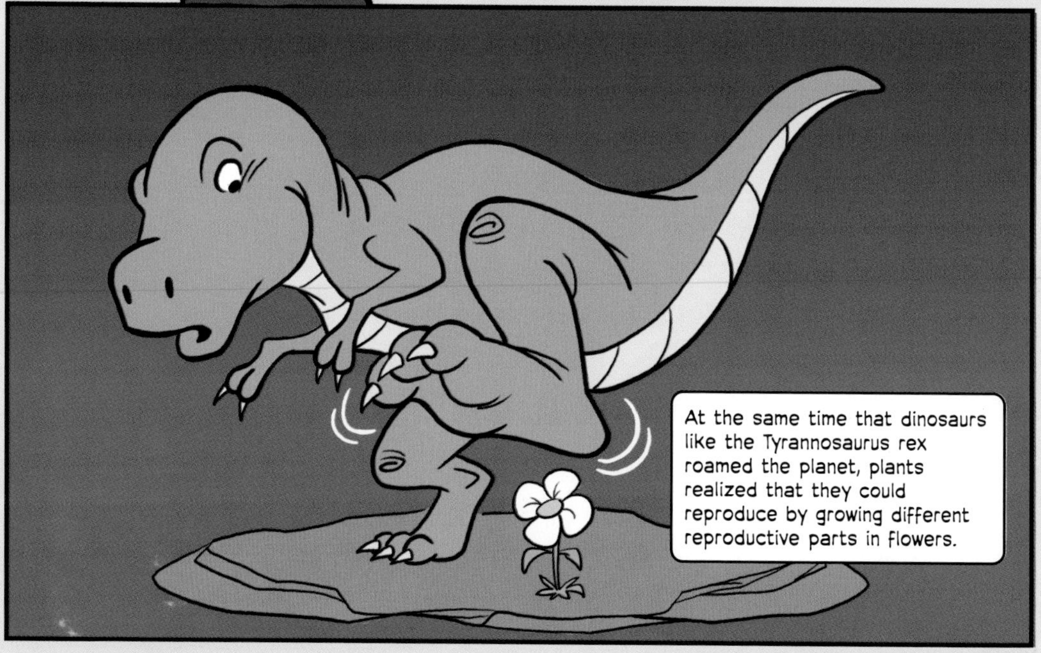
At the same time that dinosaurs like the Tyrannosaurus rex roamed the planet, plants realized that they could reproduce by growing different reproductive parts in flowers.

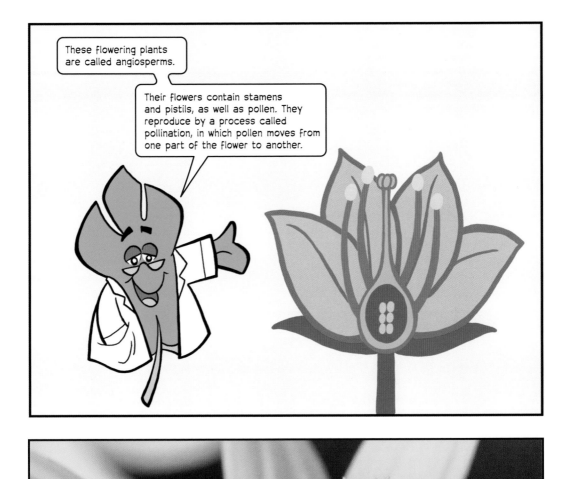

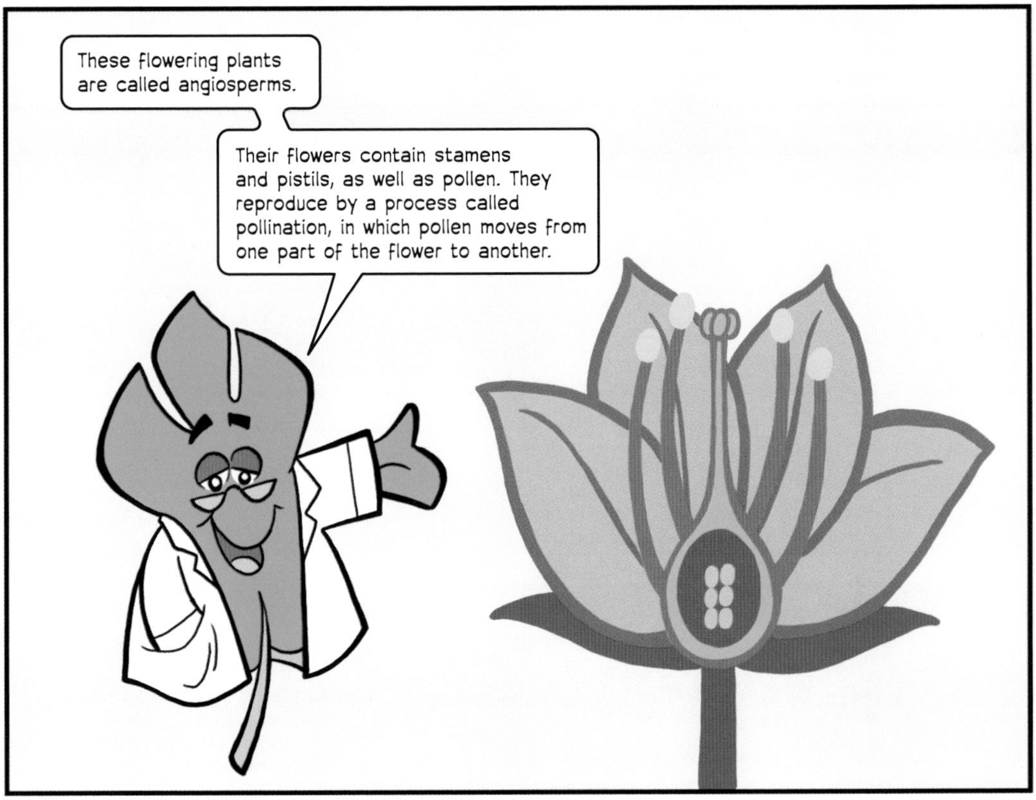
These flowering plants are called angiosperms.
Their flowers contain stamens and pistils, as well as pollen. They reproduce by a process called pollination, in which pollen moves from one part of the flower to another.

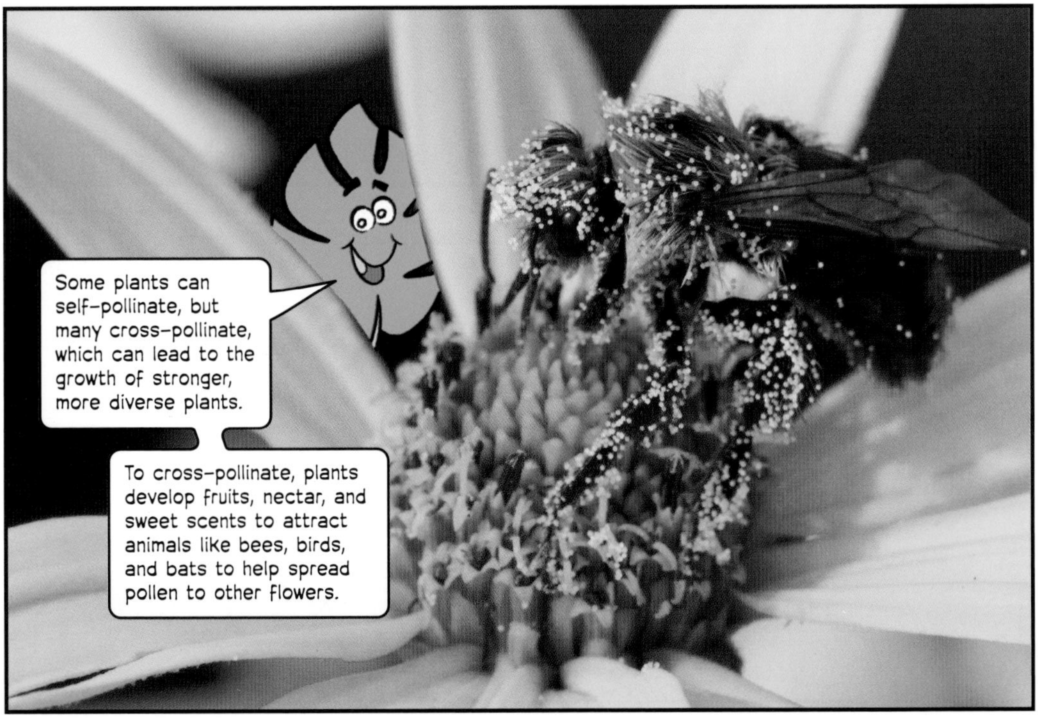
Some plants can self-pollinate, but many cross-pollinate, which can lead to the growth of stronger, more diverse plants.
To cross-pollinate, plants develop fruits, nectar, and sweet scents to attract animals like bees, birds, and bats to help spread pollen to other flowers.

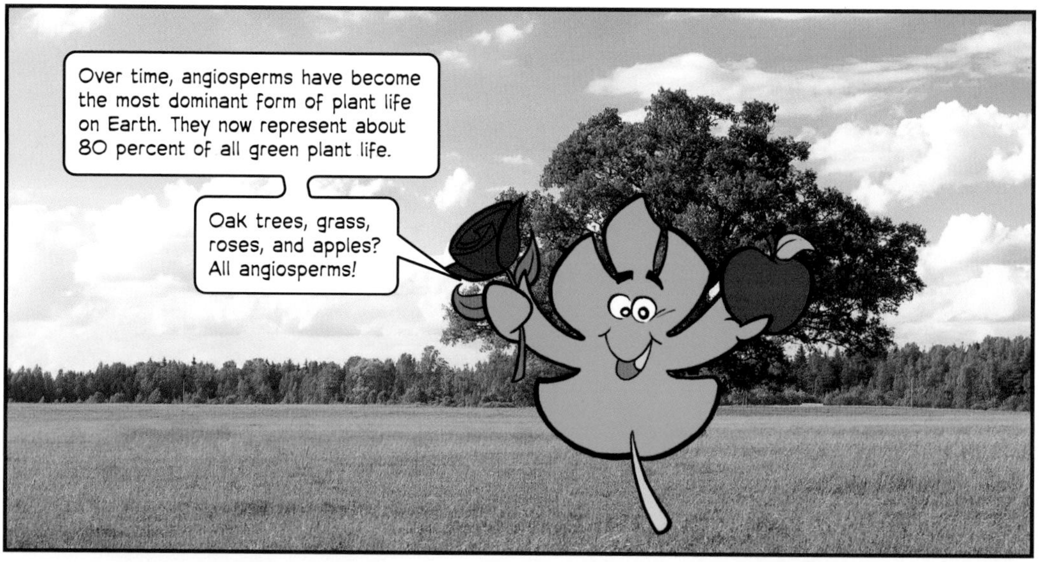
Over time, angiosperms have become the most dominant form of plant life on Earth. They now represent about 80 percent of all green plant life.
Oak trees, grass, roses, and apples? All angiosperms!

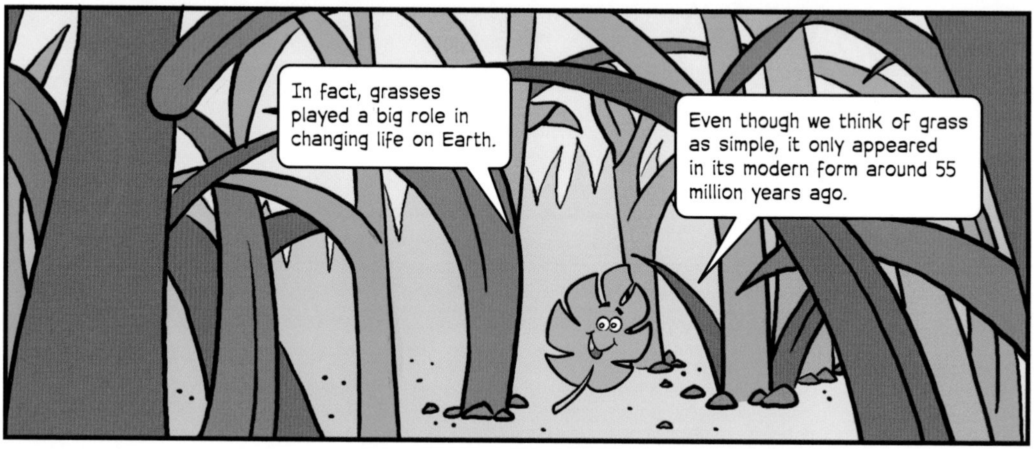
In fact, grasses played a big role in changing life on Earth.
Even though we think of grass as simple, it only appeared in its modern form around 55 million years ago.

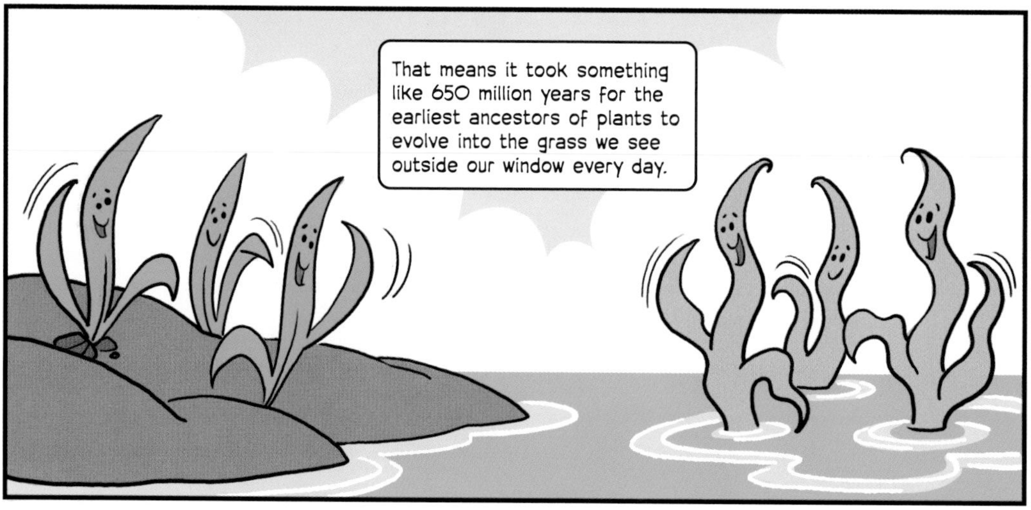
That means it took something like 650 million years for the earliest ancestors of plants to evolve into the grass we see outside our window every day.

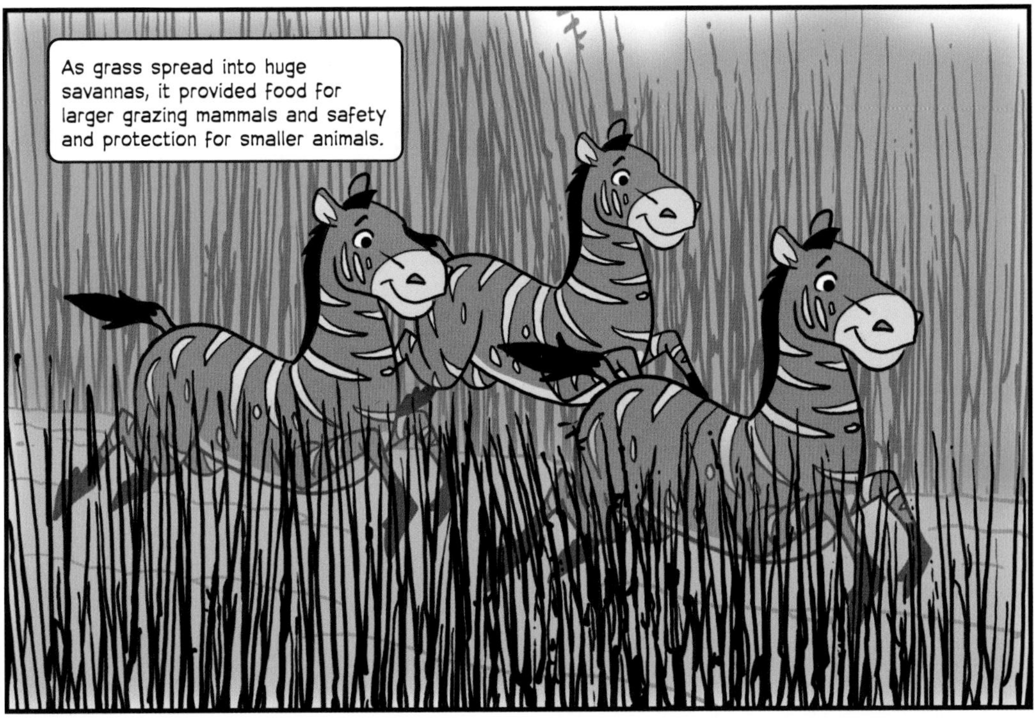
As grass spread into huge savannas, it provided food for larger grazing mammals and safety and protection for smaller animals.

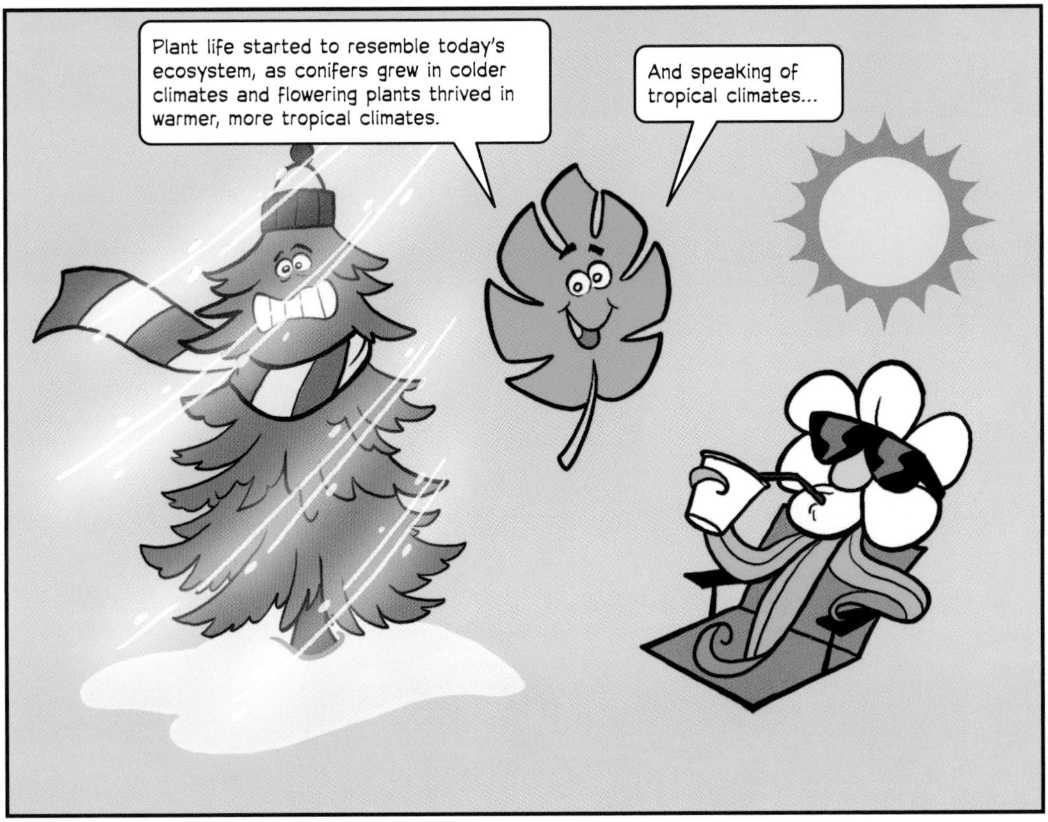
Plant life started to resemble today's ecosystem, as conifers grew in colder climates and flowering plants thrived in warmer, more tropical climates.
And speaking of tropical climates...

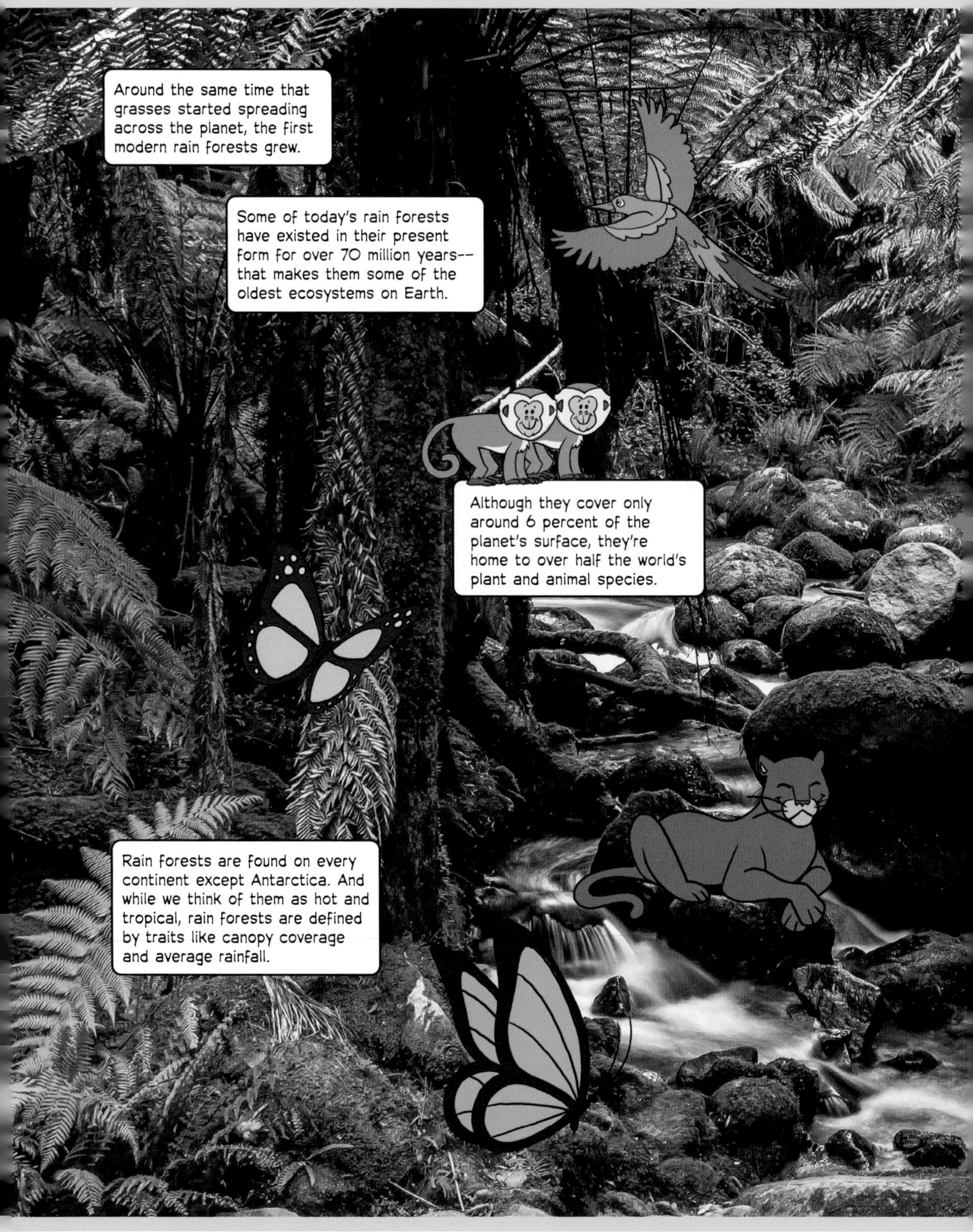
Around the same time that grasses started spreading across the planet, the first modern rain forests grew.
Some of today's rain forests have existed in their present form for over 70 million years--that makes them some of the oldest ecosystems on Earth.
Although they cover only around 6 percent of the planet's surface, they're home to over half the world's plant and animal species.
Rain forests are found on every continent except Antarctica. And while we think of them as hot and tropical, rain forests are defined by traits like canopy coverage and average rainfall.

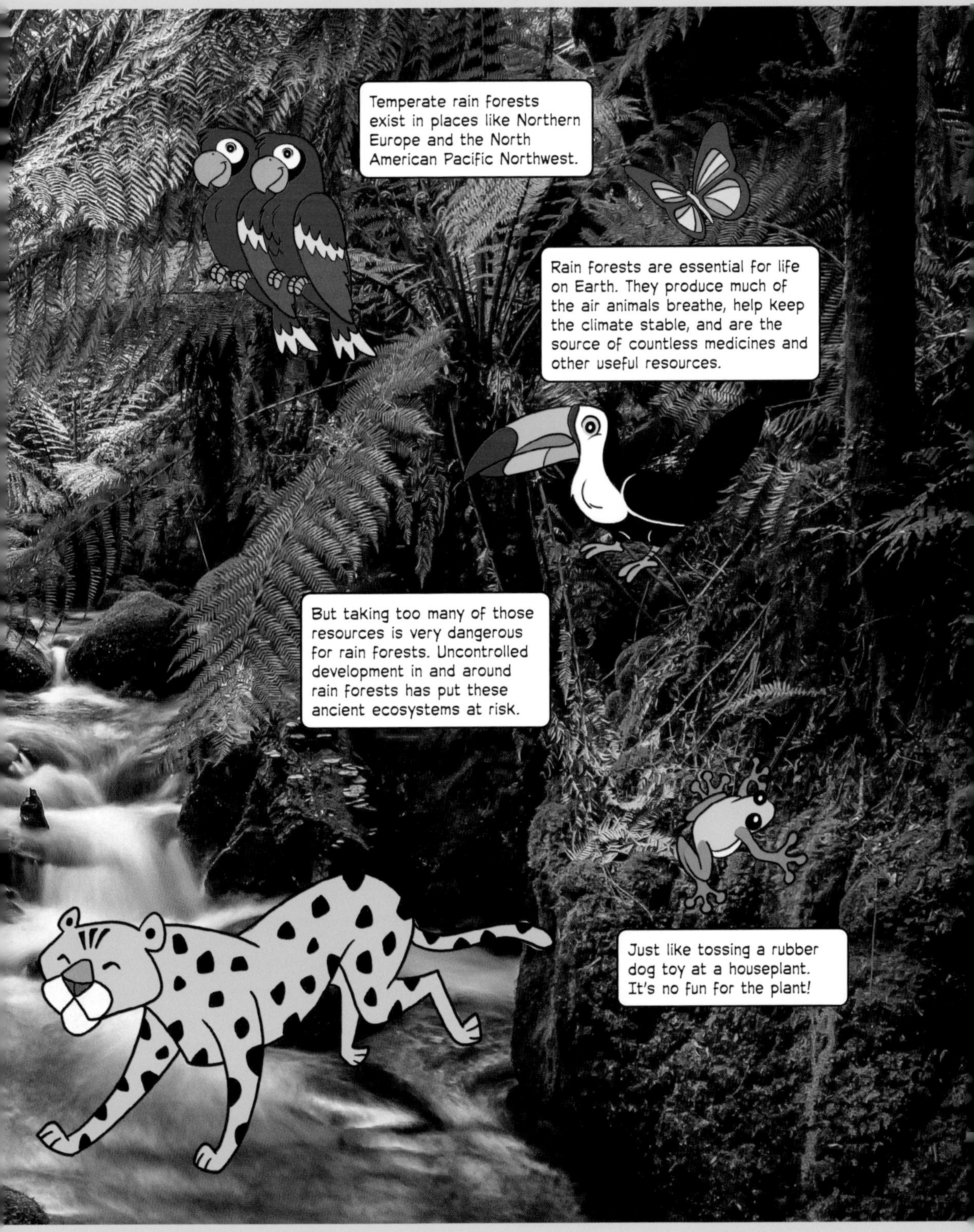
Temperate rain forests exist in places like Northern Europe and the North American Pacific Northwest.
Rain forests are essential for life on Earth. They produce much of the air animals breathe, help keep the climate stable, and are the source of countless medicines and other useful resources.
But taking too many of those resources is very dangerous for rain forests. Uncontrolled development in and around rain forests has put these ancient ecosystems at risk.
Just like tossing a rubber dog toy at a houseplant. It's no fun for the plant!

Chapter 5: AGRICULTURE

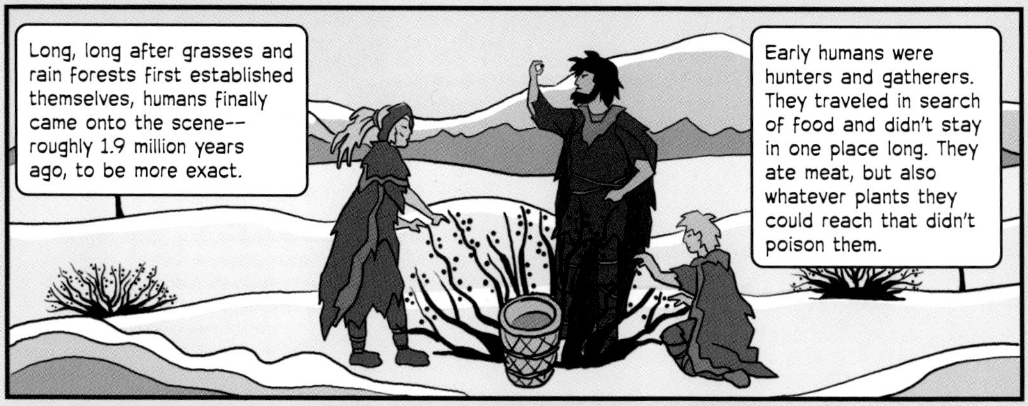

Long, long after grasses and rain forests first established themselves, humans finally came onto the scene-- roughly 1.9 million years ago, to be more exact.
Early humans were hunters and gatherers. They traveled in search of food and didn't stay in one place long. They ate meat, but also whatever plants they could reach that didn't poison them.

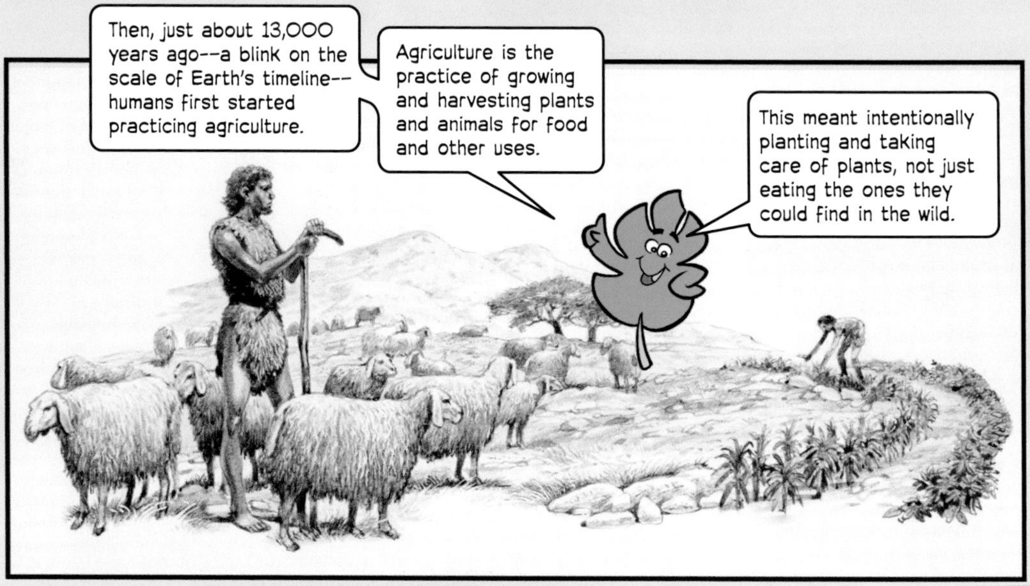

Then, just about 13,000 years ago--a blink on the scale of Earth's timeline-- humans first started practicing agriculture.
Agriculture is the practice of growing and harvesting plants and animals for food and other uses.
This meant intentionally planting and taking care of plants, not just eating the ones they could find in the wild.

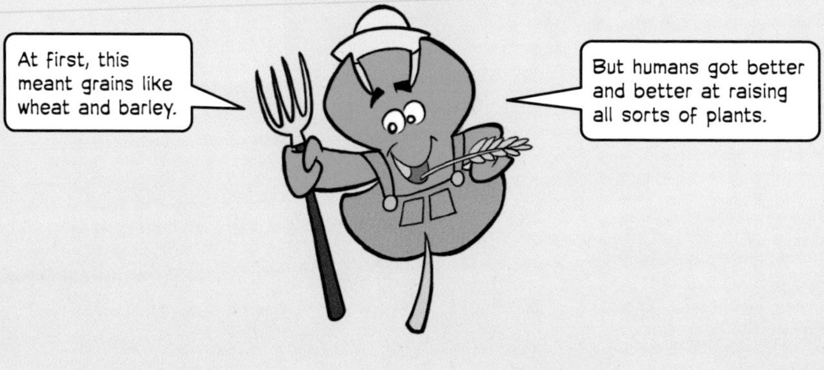

At first, this meant grains like wheat and barley.
But humans got better and better at raising all sorts of plants.

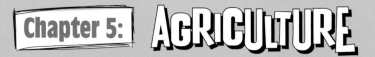

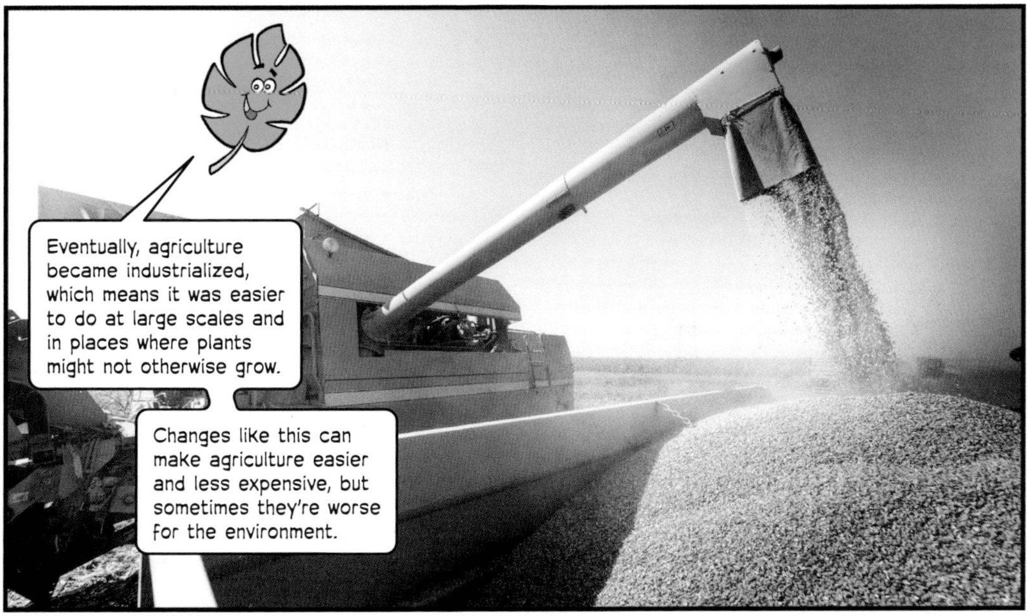
Eventually, agriculture became industrialized, which means it was easier to do at large scales and in places where plants might not otherwise grow.
Changes like this can make agriculture easier and less expensive, but sometimes they're worse for the environment.

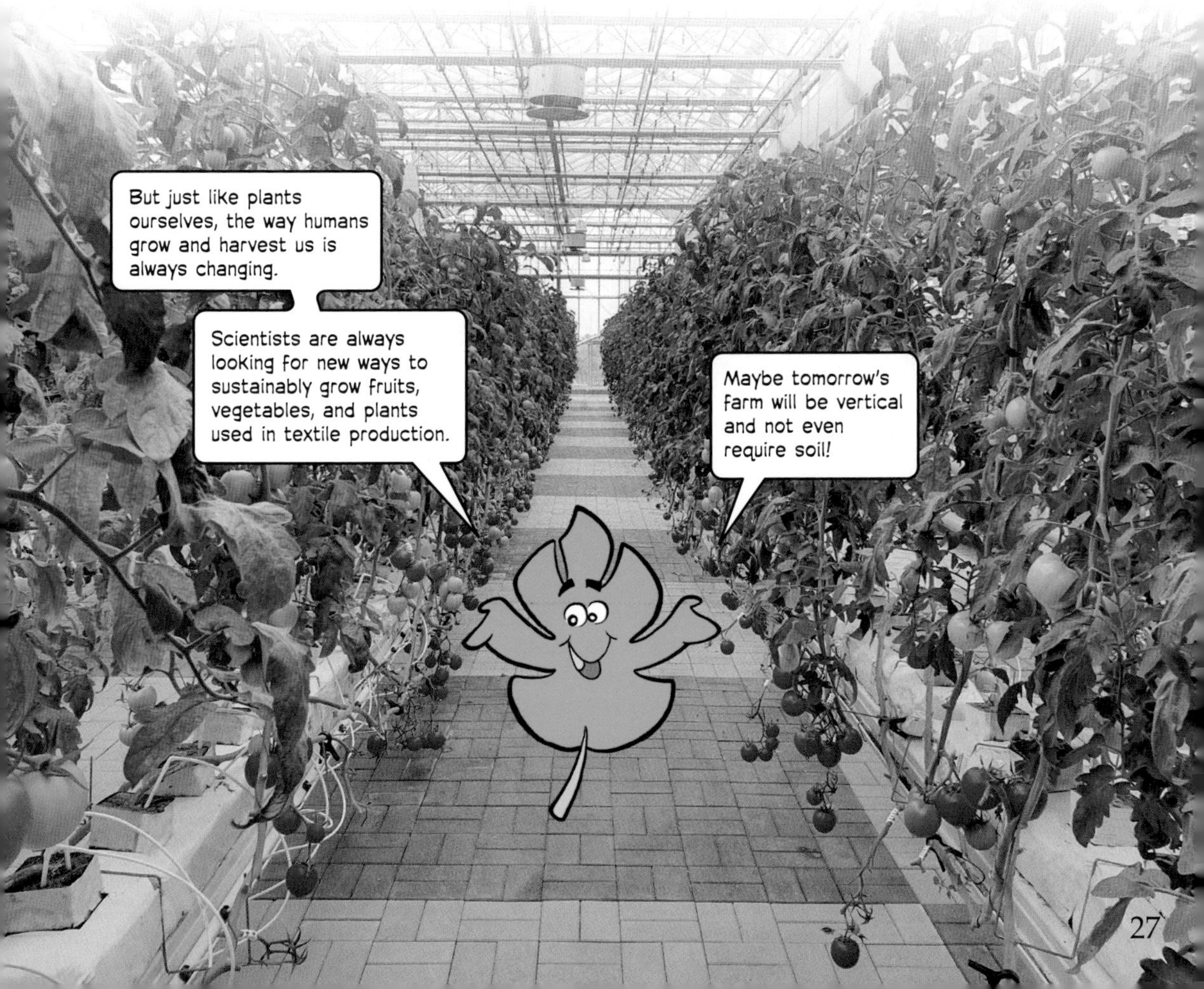
But just like plants ourselves, the way humans grow and harvest us is always changing.
Scientists are always looking for new ways to sustainably grow fruits, vegetables, and plants used in textile production.
Maybe tomorrow's farm will be vertical and not even require soil!

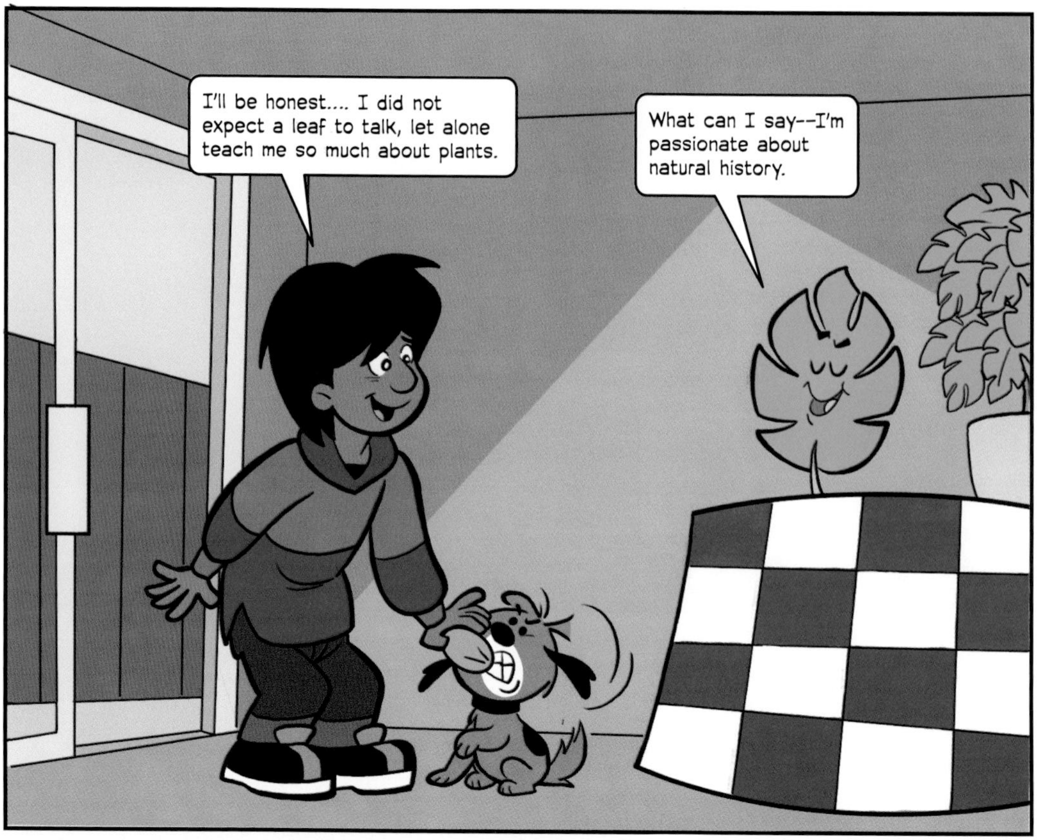
I'll be honest.... I did not expect a leaf to talk, let alone teach me so much about plants.
What can I say--I'm passionate about natural history.

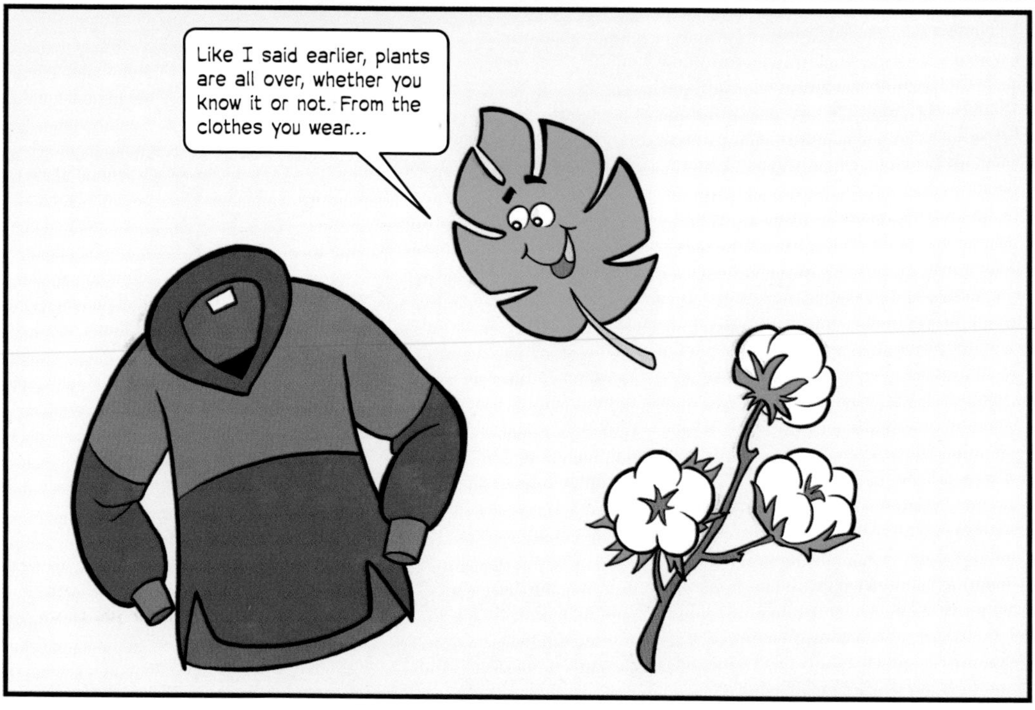
Like I said earlier, plants are all over, whether you know it or not. From the clothes you wear...

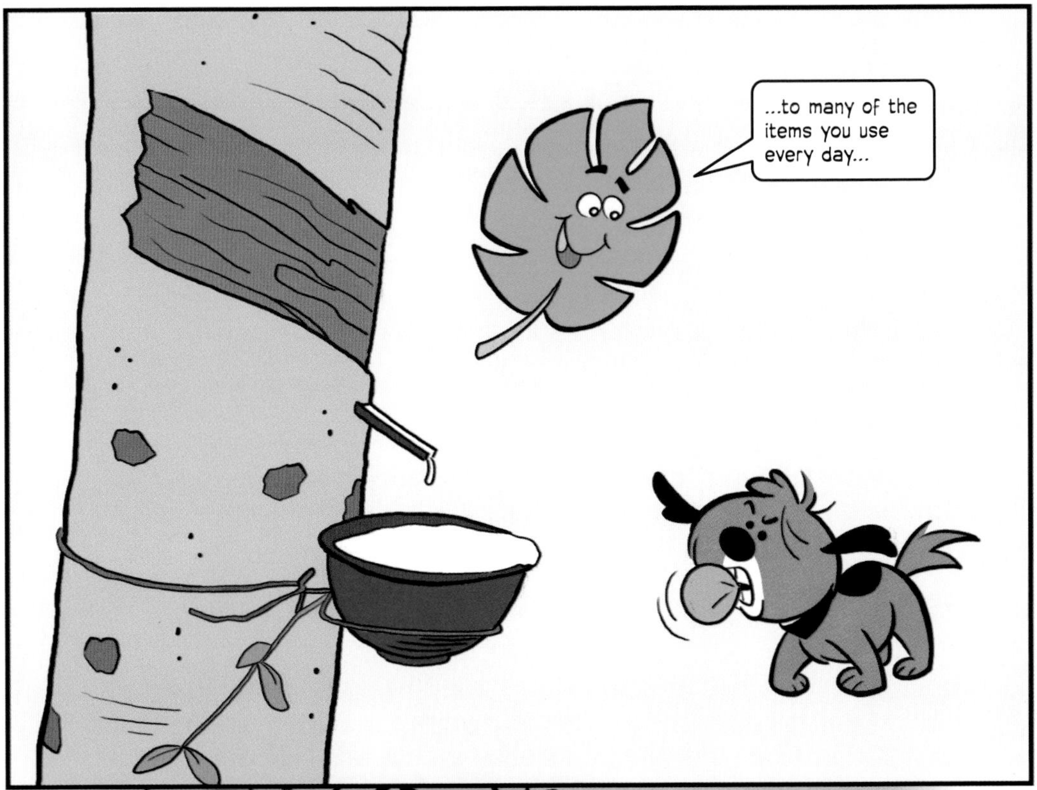
...to many of the items you use every day...

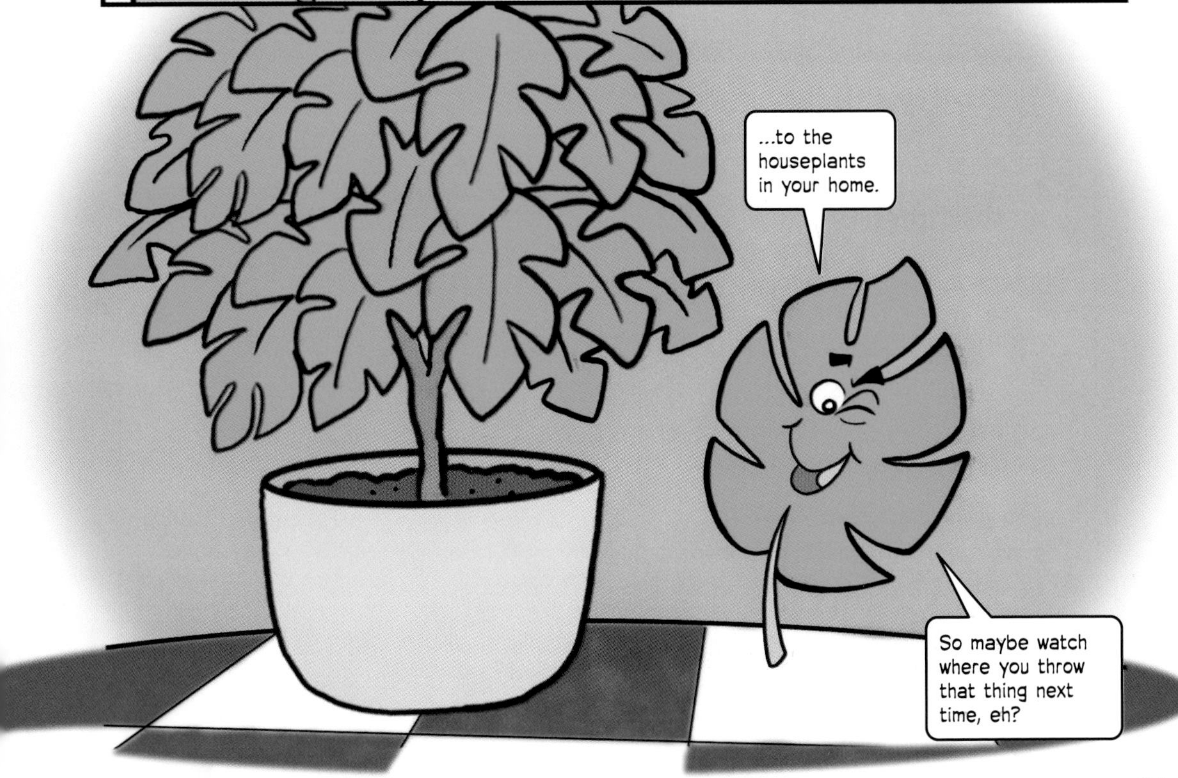
...to the houseplants in your home.
So maybe watch where you throw that thing next time, eh?

GLOSSARY

agriculture (AG-rih-kuhl-chur)—the science or occupation of cultivating the soil, producing crops, and raising livestock

carbon dioxide (KAR-buhn dye-OK-syd)—a heavy colorless gas that does not support burning, dissolves in water to form carbonic acid, is formed especially by the burning and breaking down of organic substances

cuticle (KYOO-tih-kuhl)—a thin continuous fatty or waxy film on the external surface of many higher plants

ecosystem (EE-koh-sihs-tuhm)—a system made up of an ecological community of living things interacting with their environment especially under natural conditions

germination (JUR-mih-nay-shun)—the act of sprouting or developing, as in plants

mammal (MAM-uhl)—any of a class of warm-blooded vertebrates that include human beings and all other animals that nourish their young with milk produced by mammary glands and have the skin usually more or less covered with hair

ozone layer (OH-zown LAY-ur)—a layer of the earth's atmosphere at heights of about 20 to 30 miles (32 to 48 kilometers) that is normally characterized by high ozone content that blocks most of the sun's ultraviolet radiation from entry into the lower atmosphere

photosynthesis (foh-toh-SYN-thuh-sis)— the process by which plants that contain chlorophyll make carbohydrates from water and from carbon dioxide in the air in the presence of light

prehistoric (pre-hih-STOR-ik)—of, relating to, or existing in times before written history

radiation (ray-dee-AY-shuhn)—the process of giving off radiant energy in the form of waves or particles

spore (SPOR)—a reproductive body that is produced by fungi and by some plants and microorganisms (as ferns and bacteria) and that usually consists of a single cell

vascular plant (VAS-kyoo-lur PLANT)—a plant having a specialized system for carrying fluids that includes xylem and phloem

READ MORE

Bloom, Molly, et al. *Brains On! Presents...Road Trip Earth: Explore Our Awesome Planet, from Core to Shore and So Much More.* New York: Little, Brown, 2022.

Eboch, M. M. *Forest Biomes Around the World.* North Mankato, MN: Capstone, 2020.

Hirsch, Andy. *Science Comics: Trees: Kings of the Forest.* New York: First Second, 2018.

INTERNET SITES

Britannica Kids: Plant
kids.britannica.com/students/article/plant/276449

DK Findout!: Plants
dkfindout.com/us/animals-and-nature/plants

National Geographic Kids: Facts About the Earth
natgeokids.com/uk/discover/science/space/facts-about-the-earth

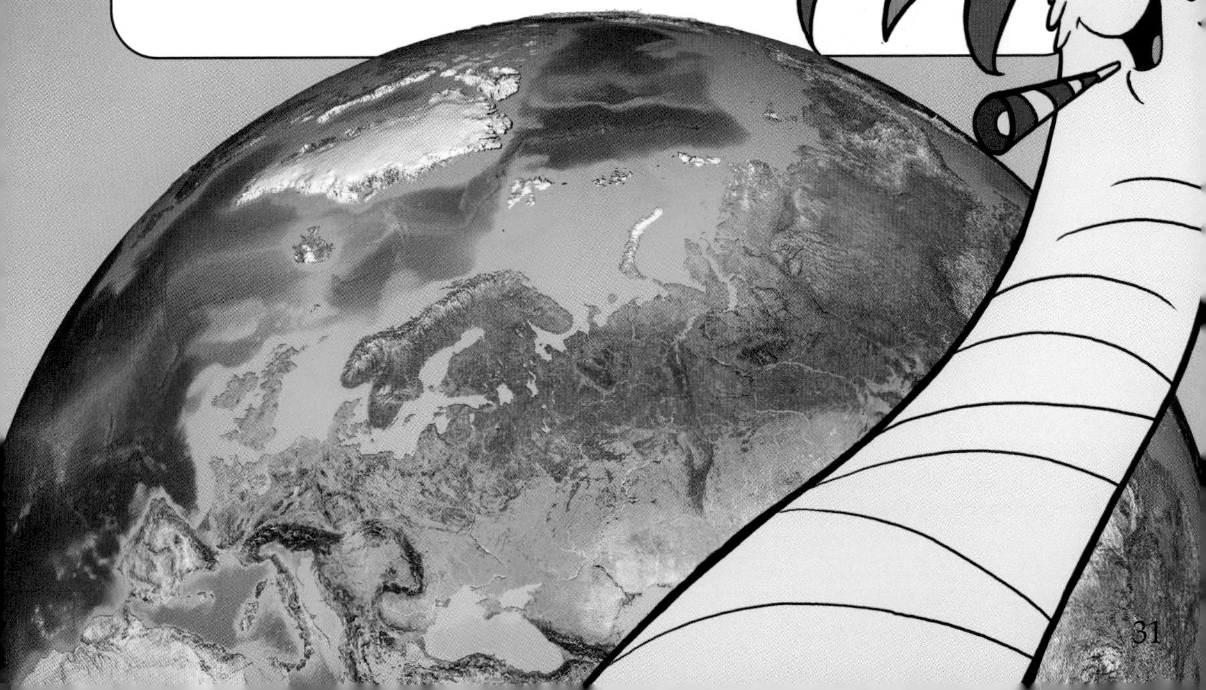

ABOUT THE AUTHOR

Steve Foxe is the Eisner Award-nominated author of over 75 comics and children's books including *X-Men '92: House of XCII*, *Rainbow Bridge*, *Adventure Kingdom*, the Spider-Ham series from Scholastic, and many works for older readers. He lives somewhere cold and exclusively eats plants. (Thanks, plants.)

ABOUT THE ILLUSTRATOR

Scott Jeralds has created many a smash hit, working in animation for Marvel Studios, Hanna-Barbera Studios, MGM Animation, Warner Bros., and PorchLight Entertainment. His TV series credits include *The Flintstones*, *Scooby-Doo*, *Superman*, *Tom and Jerry*, *The Secret Saturdays*, and more. In addition, Scott directed the cartoon series *Freakazoid!*, for which he earned an Emmy Award.